I DIDN'T CHOOSE THIS JOB,
IT CHOSE ME

Charleston, SC
www.PalmettoPublishing.com

I Didn't Choose This Job, It Chose Me
Copyright © 2021 by Brian J. Tally

First Edition

Hardcover ISBN: 978-1-63837-607-1
Paperback ISBN: 978-1-63837-608-8
eBook ISBN: 978-1-63837-609-5

I DIDN'T CHOOSE THIS JOB, IT CHOSE ME

BRIAN J. TALLY

CHIEF EDDIE GALLAGHER —

CANT EVEN BEGIN TO EXPRESS THANK. THE GRATITUDE I HAVE RIGHT NOW. MY PODCAST. ON SO MUCH FOR JOINING ME ON HAS DEDICATED YOU'RE AN INCREDIBLE MAN WHO FOR WARFIGHTERS THIS LIFE TO SERVICE. I'AM THANKFUL TO CARRY AND ALPHA MALES SUCH AS YOURSELF FASHION. THE TORCH OF LIBERTY IN AN HONORABLE SON SOON THE NEXT TORCH WILL BE PASSED TO YOUR PIG AS THE NEXT GENERATION OF WARFIGHTERS FOR AND TAKE THERE POSITION!! THANK YOU OVER THE INSPIRATION AND ENCOURAGEMENT TO THE YEARS, I'VE ALWAYS WANTED TO TELL YOU THAT LIKE MANY AMERICANS, BUT NOW I CAN. I'M THANKFUL! THANK YOU FOR AN HONORABLE + SELFLESS CAREER — ANCHORS AWEIGH SEMPER FIDELIS BRIAN TALLY

CONTENTS

FOREWORD

I JOINED THE UNITED STATES MARINE CORPS IN 1995 AFTER GRADUATing high school. After completing boot camp, it was time for combat training at Camp Pendleton in California. This is where I met Brian for the first time. During our enlistment, we would serve together in Okinawa, Korea, and Camp Pendleton.

Fast-forward several years after we both had gotten out of Marine Corps, and I reconnected with Brian through social media. We stayed in contact like this for quite some time. It was easy to see him and his family growing over the years and the great father and husband he had become. Although we lived a considerable distance apart, it was easy to stay connected. Brian is an inspiration and an example to everyone.

I had the benefit of not just reading this book but being a part of the journey. This book covers Brian's journey starting from his first trip to the emergency room to him having bills passed through Congress and eventually signed into law by President Trump.

I had the opportunity and the pleasure to help Brian with his mission. I was able to accompany Brian to Washington, DC, on two separate occasions to meet with the VA, VA committees, senators, representatives, and various news outlets and media.

I supported Brian and watched him devote his life to this mission— and he never once wavered regardless of every setback he faced. Brian's perseverance, resilience, and dedication throughout all of this are what gives this book meaning.

We are all dealt a different hand in life. It is what we choose to do with what we are given that defines us. Brian could have easily given up in a situation that many others would have. Sure, he now has a plethora of physical disabilities and the limitations that come with them, but he has not let them slow him down a bit.

I hope that this book inspires each person that reads it. Brian and his family suffered tremendously, and he will forever live with this.

Sincerely,
John Steelman / US Marine Veteran

INTRODUCTION:

My story began in Youngstown, Ohio back in 1977. I was the oldest of two boys, and to say that my brother and I had a unique childhood growing up, that would be a huge understatement. We grew up in a single parent household with our mom as our sole provider. She worked several jobs to keep food on the table, and she did a great job keeping us kids clothed, bathed, and cared for. At three years old my mom, brother and I boarded a plane for San Diego California, and we never looked back. This is where I spent my childhood running the sunny streets of San Diego, skating, surfing, playing sports, collecting baseball cards and hiking the area canyons. Just kids being kids and always getting into mischief. We were not bad kids; we were just kids with all the freedom in the world to do what we wanted so at times we found ourselves in trouble or running to get out of it. My childhood consisted of moving every year from apartment to apartment, new schools, playing baseball, and growing up quickly as I became the man of the house at an exceedingly early age. We eventually ended up in Woodland Park, Colorado at the beginning of my high school years. That was a big move for my brother and I going from the beaches of San Diego to the mountains of central Colorado and going to school with a wide variety of folks to include cowboys. It was a culture shock to say the least, but my brother and I fit in well. It ended up being a great move for the family.

Early on I never had a father to teach me "manly" things like working on cars, how to hunt, fish, and shoot or to even ride a bike. I did however end up learning a great variety of skills and different trades after we moved to Colorado, that would eventually set me up to start my own landscape construction business years later down the road.

Most of everything I have done in my life was self-taught through trial and error. But I knew one thing was certain, I watched how many men treated my mom in my early years, and I promised myself I would never treat women that way. I would always respect women and treat them with respect and dignity. I also promised myself that I would never abandon my children or family, and I would be the best husband and father I could possibly be and give my family everything that I never had. This is what gave me the drive I needed to succeed in life.

As I got closer to graduating high school, I was lost, and confused on what I should do with my life. I did not know what I wanted to be when I grew up, and time was not on my side. I was not going to sit around and wait for something to fall in my lap. I knew that would not put me on the path I wanted to be on and that was the path of success. I began searching for meaning, and purpose but I did not know how to get there, and college would not even be a consideration as my grades were not the best. I began to entertain the idea of the military and serving my country. I come from a long line of family who honorably served in the military. My family relatives have served in every war and conflict since the 'Korean War' all the way through 'Operation Enduring Freedom'.

After I saw my recruiter walk the halls of my high school with confidence, and discipline I knew that would be a great fit for me. The decision was an easy one for me. I would soon earn the title, Marine, and would be sent off to uphold and defend the constitution of the United States of America and serve my country with pride!

CHAPTER 1:

THE NIGHT FROM HELL

My name is Brian Tally, and I was living the American dream: a beautiful and devoted wife of over twenty years, a family man blessed with four incredibly talented and wonderful children. We were the owners of several small successful businesses in Colorado and California. I was a contributor to society and a man with an entrepreneurial spirit and mindset. I was doing everything right, the way  our country intended good solid American citizens to live and provide honorably for their families. A life of productivity, contribution, and hard work. A thirty-eight-year-old man that seemed to have it all figured out as life generously rained blessings upon my family and me for decades.

A dedicated and committed husband and father, a coach, a role model, a friend, a son, a brother, an uncle, a nephew, a cousin, your neighbor, and a proud US Marine veteran that honorably served our great nation. Then out of nowhere, and without warning, came that fateful morning that I will never forget. My life would be turned upside down and I would soon be faced with adversity in a way that most will never experience in a lifetime. My life was about to change in ways that I could never see coming or ever imagine.

My story reads like a book and plays out like a movie that is so horrific, egregious, and inhumane that most audiences would believe it to be fiction. It all began in January of 2016 with grueling night sweats that soaked my sheets as I tossed and turned, fighting this sudden onset of back pain that was unexplainable because I had not suffered any injuries or trauma.

As the torment continued, it brought me out of my bed and directly onto my knees as I slowly crawled to the bathroom floor where I laid moaning, groaning, and sobbing facedown on the cold bathroom tiles and rolling back and forth on the floor. I did everything I could possibly do to find any relief and was immediately desperate for answers. The discomfort and pain rapidly grew from severe to relentless to indescribable excruciating agony.

I could no longer walk, the sweat began to flow like a water faucet, and my bladder was extremely full. I could not stand up to urinate, so I reached for a bucket near my bathtub where I positioned myself to the side and tried to relieve myself so the painful stomach cramping and bladder pain would stop. That was the first time I experienced bladder paralysis; it took several hours to empty my bladder as it dripped into a bucket where I cried myself to sleep as I was completely worn down physically, mentally, and emotionally after an awfully long and taxing night.

Several hours later I woke up with a mess, a bucket half full of urine, as I laid in a small puddle of my own pee. At that time, I crawled and shuffled my way back into my room and woke up my wife, Jenny, and explained to her that I was in dire need of help and begged her to immediately take me to the emergency room. She woke up startled, shocked, scared, and surprised by what I was trying to explain to her as I was now having a hard time even speaking due to the pain, slurred speech, and fatigue my body was experiencing.

Without delay my wife loaded me into the car with help from my children and sped off to the emergency room. The car ride to the ER felt as if it took a lifetime to get there. I was in bad shape, reclined all the way back in the seat, moaning, as I just tossed and turned, moving my legs back and forth, doing everything I conceivably could do to fight this immense onslaught of pain. As a veteran I had my health care through the Department of Veterans Affairs (VA), so my wife drove to the nearest emergency room, which was in nearby Loma Linda, California.

I had always had good and acceptable care at the VA and never really experienced any major issues except for the long process of making and scheduling appointments and waiting on hold sometimes for hours on end. But once you were in the system and present at your scheduled appointments, everything seemed to run as well as it should.

Obviously with any health care these days, there are pluses and minuses and will always be room for improvement; however, the decision to go to the VA emergency room on that cold and gloomy January morning in Southern California would end up being the worst decision and the greatest mistake of my life.

CHAPTER 2:
THE DREADED EMERGENCY ROOM VISIT

INALLY, AFTER A LONG AND PAINFUL CAR RIDE, WE ARRIVED AT THE Loma Linda VA emergency room. My wife checked me in and explained my sudden onset of pain and the symptoms I was showing and outlined in detail what I was going through, experiencing, and further described this as nothing less than a critical state, and I was in need of emergency care, and attention was promptly needed.

Shortly thereafter I was triaged by two emergency room nurse clinicians. I was given an x-ray and several injections of painkillers to include Toradol, Kenalog, and Methocarbamol. I was diagnosed with a low back sprain and prescribed an overabundance of pills to include opioids, muscle relaxers, anxiety medications, nerve pain medications, and a variety of nonsteroidal anti-inflammatories.

During that visit I never saw a doctor, I was denied a simple blood test, and I was also denied an MRI that my wife had requested to find the answers we needed. Having never gone through an experience such as the one that was now before us, we thought this was standard protocol. I was sent home with instructions to rest, stretch, take the medications that were prescribed to me, and follow up with my primary care physician (PCP).

The number of medications that were prescribed to me on that first trip to the emergency room was alarming. It filled up a large VA pharmacy bag. As I was being wheeled out to the car to head home, I wasted no time in opening all of the medications and began taking my prescribed regimen. I just wanted the pain to go away. Soon after, I started to feel numb from the pain, as the medicine was all beginning to settle in. Even though I could still feel the pain physically, my mind did not seem to care mentally. All at the same time, my body was throbbing, and pain was radiating up and down my spine and down through my legs.

The best way to describe the pain and sensation is it felt like I was being stabbed with an ice pick in and out of my spine, lower back, and buttocks. I also felt a sharp needle sensation that would send a feeling of being shocked and poked with needles down my legs and buttocks. It was the strangest feeling in the world, but now that I had sought some relief from the pain and the symptoms were being masked, my mind immediately went into a state of physical and emotional detachment.

Once I got home, I was unable to walk, so I was carefully led upstairs and directly to the recliner in my room. I still remember being woken up every four to six hours by my wife as I was in and out of sedation and given a handful of pills and a glass of water. I did not have an appetite, so after each pill session, I would doze off for hours on end until being woken up for my next cocktail of prescription drugs or when I needed to use the restroom.

I was having an extremely hard time using the bathroom because I did not have a steady flow when urinating. It would slowly drip out, and I was not in shape to stand or even sit down on the toilet. So, my wife brought me a bucket, and when I needed to go, I would very carefully slide out of my recliner and straddle myself over the bucket, all while leaning the rest of my body over the recliner and burying my head directly into the top portion of the chair as I dripped into the bucket. I was doing everything I could possibly do to help take my mind off this torment as I was living in misery, and it felt so egregious and painful.

I began concentrating on the neighborhood dogs that were barking, the sounds of the wind blowing in through a small crack in my bedroom window, the loud mufflers on cars, the screeching of tires in my neighborhood, and the smells of food being made by neighbors filling the air with a nice aroma. I was searching for some sort of connectivity to the outside world.

I would be straddled in this position typically for about forty-five minutes at a time to completely empty my bladder. When I was finished, I would slide the bucket to the side of my chair and very carefully climb back into the recliner, all  while suffering excruciating back spasms and cramps from making even the slightest of movements as my body began to enter a state of atrophy.

Other times I would fall asleep in this position, laid up on the floor directly in front of my recliner, and later be woken up by my wife to help me get back into my chair so she could empty the bucket and reload me with my cocktail of powerful drugs.

CHAPTER 3:

BAD TO WORSE

For the next several days, my wife spent literally every waking moment on the phone trying to track down my VA primary care physician (PCP) as ordered to do by the ER triage clinicians upon my discharge for a follow-up visit. After two days of unreturned phone calls and messages to my PCP after my initial emergency room visit, things went from really bad to worse very quickly.

My wife loaded me into the car and drove me right back where we originally started, the VA Loma Linda. I was now so severely drugged up and in a state of incapacitation, suffering continued unspeakable and immeasurable pain unlike anything I have ever experienced in my entire life. I showed up displaying the same exact symptoms that I had just days before, but now I was in a wheelchair. While I was waiting to be seen, the pain became the worst I had experienced up to this point and became so unbearable I began having a severe panic attack in the emergency room. I slid out of my chair and onto the floor and balled up into a fetal-like position and was in complete and utter panic mode.

For the second time in two days, I was once again in immediate need of emergency care. My wife began to cry and plead for help as she yelled, "He's dying—please help my husband!" She was being consoled by several other veterans in the waiting room. Once the triage nurses took notice and remembered us from the day's past, they began to yell at my wife for bringing me back to the emergency room without first following up with my VA PCP. My wife explained that she could not get through and reach the PCP after countless calls and messages into the VA Murrieta Clinic. Aside from the indescribable pain, my symptoms continued to worsen with profuse sweating, body aches, and slurred speech, along with the inability to use the restroom effectively.

These were some of the biggest red flags that I exhibited and the reason why my wife brought me back to the ER in a desperate plea to find the emergency help I needed. The triage nurses triaged me once again, gave me two injections of Dilaudid for the panic and pain, and diagnosed me with the same diagnosis as before, a sprained and strained lower back.

The nurse repeatedly said the x-ray was normal and showed no signs of a problem. My wife then asked for a second time in as many days to see a doctor and order an MRI or some sort of diagnostic testing and a blood test. We were denied once again the requests made by my wife.

We were discharged with additional prescription drugs and sent home with instructions to follow up with my PCP. The clinicians had once again treated my symptoms and masked the pain with powerful narcotics and did not explore any further options. The following day my PCP finally called my wife back, and they were now in communication. That gave us some hope that I would at the very least see a doctor for the first time since this all began and try to get some much needed and well-deserved answers.

Regrettably, she could not schedule an appointment to see me due to her schedule already being overbooked; however, she did agree to meet with me for a brief minute in passing between her appointments, and she quickly concluded that my back was sprained, agreed with the initial ER reports, and diagnosed me with a low back sprain. I was instructed to stretch and take it easy for a few weeks and was told that I should start feeling better soon.

My wife was upset with the lack of care and compassion and pleaded one final time for an MRI and respectfully asked that they run some tests. Unfortunately, our repeated requests were denied once again, and we were told that my condition and diagnosis did not warrant any additional testing other than the original x-ray that was taken on my initial emergency room visit.

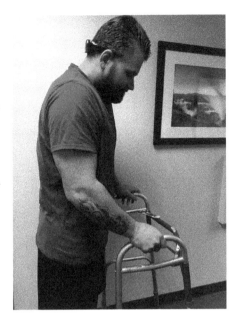

I was in unbelievably bad shape and visibly extremely sick; I was using a walker and at times was in a wheelchair as I could barely hold myself up. We accepted my PCP's final diagnosis and thought that we were as proactive as possible and following protocol. We took the advice of my PCP and went home to rest and continued with my prescribed cocktail of pills every four to six hours.

Soon thereafter, as I lay dying in my chair, I began to feel myself slip away physically, mentally, and emotionally. I was trapped in a whirlwind of nightmares with no way out. My body was riddled with severe anxiety and

depression fueled by physical pain and fear of the unknown, at the lowest and most terrifying time in my life. I was hopeless, helpless, and felt

13

as if I were a prisoner in my own home, desperately waiting for my next handful of pills to seek much-needed relief.

My life as I once knew it had rapidly and radically changed literally overnight, and I had no idea what in the hell had just hit me, let alone what was even going on.

CHAPTER 4:
ENOUGH IS ENOUGH

Several weeks went by, and I was literally deteriorating right before our very eyes. I was down nearly forty pounds and was showing no signs of improvement. The grueling night sweats continued along with urinary incontinence and hesitancy. Furthermore, my wife continuously made repeated calls and checked in with the primary care physician, offering updates, and made even more requests for an MRI and diagnostic testing. The primary care physician stated that she would put a call into ortho and investigate a possible MRI and that they would contact me if I was approved.

Well, that day never came, and finally my wife said, "Enough is enough," and she took matters into her own hands. We paid $500 dollars out of pocket for our own MRI through a private imaging facility in Temecula, California. Upon arriving at the medical center, I could not walk, so I was escorted and helped along with a wheelchair that was provided by the imaging facility. I was then placed on a cold MRI table and given some headphones. This was all entirely new to me as I had never had an MRI in my life.

The music started and it followed by the obnoxious sounds an MRI makes, full of knocking and ringing that set into my ears. The force of the noise was even rattling in my body and in my bones, making the pain and the experience that more unbearable. I was stuffed into a tube in the most painful way imaginable. I concentrated on those sounds and then out of nowhere music began to play through the headphones I was

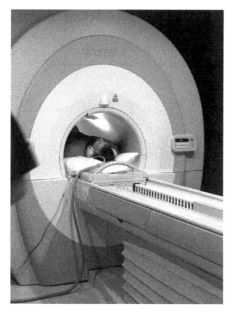

given. The song 'Slow Ride', by Foghat came on and I started to try to imagine the good times. I mean who doesn't like classic 70's rock n' roll; and for a brief second my mind was in tune with the music.

The music was a nice gesture, but I was in grave condition and could barely even make it through the MRI due to the amount of pain I was in, regardless of the high pill quantities I was taking.

After the MRI was completed, I was assisted by three clinicians that helped me off the table and I was wheeled out. Once I got back outside, I felt as if the life had been sucked out of me, however life around me continued. The sights and sounds of fast-paced traffic, the smells of flowers in bloom, the birds chirping, and the aroma of fast food filling the air as the lunch rush was in high gear. I could even remember smelling the grilled onions from a nearby In N Out burger joint.

All I could think about was my once active and outgoing self was now scooting around at a snail's pace with a wheelchair and walker. I was scared to death and had no idea what had hit me and what the hell was going on. Within a day we were given the findings of the MRI, and it showed a slew of structural problems and that I would need surgery.

The results were mind-boggling, as there was no trauma, accident, or injury that ever occurred that would lead me to an MRI finding such as the one we received. The results consisted of spinal stenosis, posterior disc bulges, increased moderate central canal stenosis, and chronic multi-level; central canal and neural foraminal stenosis. The primary diagnostic code was as follows: ABNORMALITY, ATTENTION NEEDED.

We began to scratch our heads, and we just could not comprehend what we were being told. My wife immediately hand-delivered the results of the MRI to the VA Murrieta Clinic as well as the orthopedic surgeon's office at VA Loma Linda and requested that these findings immediately get into the hands of my primary care provider and the surgeon for their review, as surgery was imminent.

Finally, after two weeks we were seen by the VA Loma Linda orthopedic department; they read the MRI and went over the findings and explained the results with my wife and me. They confirmed that I would need surgery and that there were multiple areas of structural damage in my spine. At that time, the surgeon scheduled my back surgery to take place at the VA Loma Linda surgery department on December 7, 2016. My wife and I then looked at each with utter shock and dismay as this was March 16, 2016.

For a few minutes there were no words, just a deluge of tears that immediately began flowing down my face and onto the walker I was clutching for dear life. With panic my wife began to cry, became emotional, and pleaded with the staff for an earlier date as she feared for my life, and the life of her children's father. The more and more my wife and I looked at each other from across the room, there were no words, just eye contact as the tears continued to flow.

The sound of the surgeon's assistant shuffling papers back and forth to find an earlier surgery date became more worrisome by the second, and each keystroke on the keyboard made my anxiety and fear grow immensely and was soon magnified by 1000 percent knowing that I may not be selected for surgery for nine months and there was nothing I could do about it besides take another pill, and another, and another until I couldn't feel the physical, mental, and emotional pain anymore. Becoming numb and powerless was the only option that I felt I had as every ounce of life I had in me slowly began to bleed out.

My mind never stopped thinking; I was reliving precious moments of my past shared with my children and wife, friends, events, life, love, laughter, and joy, all while trying to figure out in my head just what the hell was going on and how did everything go south so fast.

CHAPTER 5:
VETERANS CHOICE ENROLLMENT

BY NOW SEVERAL WEEKS HAD passed. My wife, Jenny, spent every waking hour on the phone, advocating on my behalf, juggling the daily household chores, getting the kids where they needed to be, shopping, laundry, dishes, and taking care of me full-time as my caregiver.

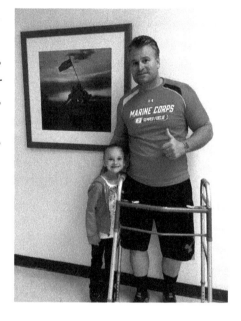

My little girl never left my side. She would sit and talk to me on my walker that she filled up with children's stickers. I told her she could decorate it as she felt fit, and from that point on she was my "ride or die." She never missed any of my appointments, and sadly most of her life has been spent growing up in hospitals and clinics and seeing her dad live a life in pain and discomfort. There is no doubt in my mind that this little girl is my angel.

Through my wife's hard work, advocacy, and tenacious efforts, we finally received a phone call that we had been anxiously awaiting. It was the VA orthopedic department, and for the first time in months we finally had some good news delivered to us as we were now approved to go outside the VA for my surgery through the Veterans Choice Program. The enrollment process was not easy. It required full-time emails, phone calls, messages, and endless paperwork. It was all done in an effort to get the surgery approved through the outside provider, get me seen and established as a new patient, and get the surgery scheduled ASAP through the outside provider. This too was a long and tiring process.

Up to this point, nothing ever came easy. Brick walls surrounded us, and literally every door we went to for help was not just closed, but we felt as if we were in a locked room with no way out. The further we went down this rabbit hole, the deeper we fell into crisis mode as a family. This egregious and unnecessary waiting game was being played out before us all while my life, health, and livelihood were all hanging in the balance. After what seemed to be a lifetime of paperwork and endless phone calls, my wife finally made some headway (bless her heart), and we were finally seen by an outside provider and met the surgeon that would be performing my back surgery.

The surgeon's staff reviewed my chart and got me scheduled for April 30, 2016, at Scripps Mercy Hospital in San Diego. Nearly five weeks later, that day arrived. It seemed as if a lifetime had passed as my family, and I counted down the days to "Daddy's" surgery. The kids even made a countdown chain, like the ones enthusiastic children make as they count down the final days until Christmas in utter joy and excitement. This is how my family and I felt heading into my surgery. At last, the day has come, and it felt as if a ton of bricks was lifted off our shoulders.

We were now four months into this atrocious story, and we were all tired and exhausted beyond belief; we were all ready to have our lives back, reinstated daily routines, and some sort of normalcy again. I was eager to roll my sleeves up again and get back to work, and I prayed to be healed and free of pain. Sitting and wasting away in a chair for nearly four months was a prison sentence in my own home. Anyone who knows me knows that I am a hardworking man that could never sit still, let alone sit down, always on the go, and a guy that got things done, provided well for his family, and always wore his heart on his sleeve. I was ready! We arrived at Scripps Hospital for the scheduled surgery feeling optimistic that this would all soon be over, and we can finally begin to start our healing process and the road to recovery.

My wife checked me in, and soon thereafter I was admitted, and the surgical staff immediately started the pre-operation process. I began to have butterflies and an overwhelming sensation of nervous jitters, and severe anxiety. That was soon eliminated after my first dose of anti-anxiety medications were fed through my IV; I immediately felt the cold sensation that made its way through my veins and felt as if I was invisible without a worry or a care in the world. I was now mentally ready for surgery. I remember my wife and children all waiting in the room with me and never leaving my side until they took me back. We said our goodbyes, and shared hugs. I could see the sadness and worry in their faces as they fought back tears. My wife and four children all gave me their blessings and we said our "I love you's." I could also sense their excitement because my wife and children would soon have their husband and father back.

The operating room was now ready for me, and I was wheeled away straight through a double set of doors. I instantly felt a cold blast of air and was lifted onto a very cold steel table. The countdown from 100 began, and before I could get to 96, I was out like a light.

CHAPTER 6:

FEARING THE WORST

THE SURGEON BEGAN WHAT HE thought was supposed to be a routine back surgery, but he soon found out why I fell gravely ill, and the reasoning on why my health rapidly declined so fast. To the surgeon's surprise as I laid open on the operating table, he found the underlying root of the problem. The surgeon best described my spinal bone, disc, and tissue as being "moth-eaten" and bursting with inflammation. Red flags went up everywhere within the operating room, and the surgeon quickly notified the infectious disease doctor of a

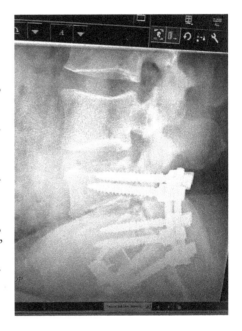

potentially life-threatening issue that was now unfolding and developing very quickly. The surgeon continued with the surgery and was assisted by the infectious disease doctor. They began cutting out infected spinal bone, disc, and tissue and replaced it all with screws and rods.

The overall length of the surgery was just over five hours. Meanwhile my family began to grow worried as the surgeon had told my wife that

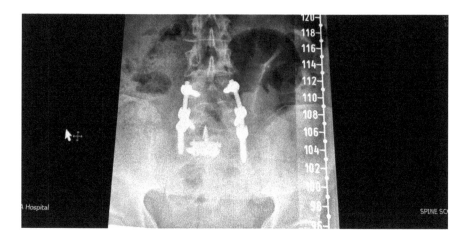

the procedure would only take three to four hours, and now they were in hour five. As their anxiety levels rose and their hearts began to race, the door that they had not taken their eyes off finally opened, and they were relieved to see the surgeon come out to update my family as to how the surgery went.

Unfortunately, they were greeted with bad news and uncertainty. The surgeon explained that my spine was in bad shape, full of inflammation and staphylococcus, a deadly bacterium. He explained that this strain of bacteria could have gotten into my bloodstream and caused sepsis—and eventually result in systemwide failure of the organs and ultimately death. The surgeon promised my family that he would get to the bottom of the underlying root of this profoundly serious problem, and he did just that.

Immediately following surgery, the surgeon ordered every test under the sun as he feared I had bone cancer and he was trying to rule out any possibility imaginable. All the while, my family, my wife and four children, were panic stricken and still waiting now very anxiously as they paced back and forth in the waiting room sharing hugs, shedding tears, and praying for a positive outcome. My wife, being the strong woman she is and the "rock" of our family, the foundation and glue if you will, rallied my children together for a brief family huddle in the waiting room, and they all promised that once they were allowed to visit me in recovery, they would act like everything went great and the surgery was a success and that it was time for me to rest and recover.

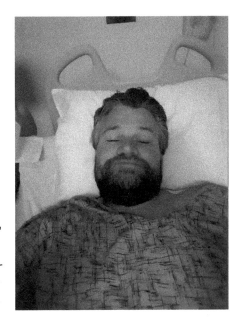

They did this to keep me at bay and to protect my mental state of mind, so I did not go into panic and worry mode, as I was already battling severe anxiety up to the point of my surgery. Plus, they felt the timing would not be right to inform me of the surgeon's findings immediately after waking up from a brutal surgery as I lay in recovery with a drain tube stuck in my back and a catheter installed with the bag in my lap.

When my family came through that door to greet me, all their tears were wiped clean, and they were all smiles, as they were offering words of encouragement as the well-wishes flowed from their grieving hearts. Shortly thereafter I was inundated with clinicians as they began poking me and forcing tiny tubes into my veins as they pulled blood and mixed it with powdery substances on trays that were parked directly in front of me. Minutes later there were even more clinicians coming into my room to perform other varieties of tests; all the while my family was telling me that these tests were all protocol, especially after having a surgery like the one I just had. They told me not to worry, so I did my best to not have a worry in the world. I was content because I had my family by my side once again, however I felt numb because of the strength and volume of prescribed narcotics that I had on a constant drip that was working in my body to combat my pain levels and anxiety.

Within thirty minutes I had a barrage of clinicians working on me, and it seemed as if they were working at a rapid pace. One of them even gave me a one-liter bottle of water mixed with a bitterly sweet potion,

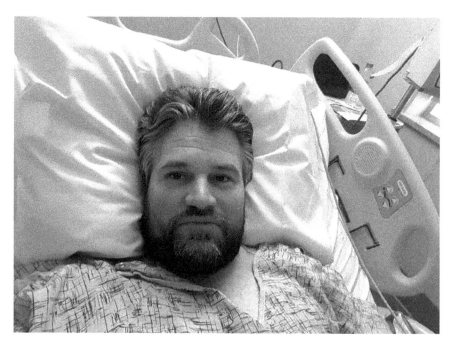

and I was instructed to drink this whole thing within an hour for a CT scan. My antennae began to go up because of all this hurried and spontaneous care I was receiving from the time I was wheeled off to what was supposed to be "recovery" but was far from recovery. For the next several hours, I was wheeled throughout the hospital and accompanied by a half dozen clinicians who represented different departments of the hospital as they led me down the hospital hallways to every diagnostic testing available. Some of the testing that was conducted was a CT scan, PET scan, ultrasounds, EKG, and a bone scan.

After the testing and the running around was complete, I returned to my room and tried to get some much-needed rest, as my body was utterly exhausted. It was now nearing midnight, my family was an emotional wreck, and they too were spent and needed some well-deserved sleep and rest of their own. My kids all took turns giving me hugs and handshakes, then my wife came in for a good night kiss, and she promised to be back first thing in the morning. "That's a wrap," I mumbled to myself as the lights went out on this long, debilitating, painful day.

CHAPTER 7:

THE DIAGNOSIS AND THE DAGGER

After a brutal night of pain and being immobilized in the hospital bed, I was extremely uncomfortable and did not get any sleep. To top it off, I had some painful tubes coming out of me that just made things difficult. Finally, daybreak came, and I was met with a nasty bowl of oatmeal and a rotten banana. "Good morning," said the charge nurse as she checked my vitals and emptied my catheter.

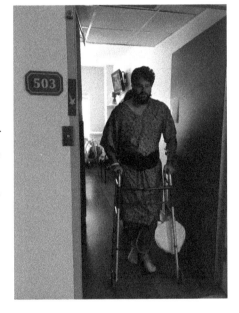

Shortly thereafter my room quickly filled with those same clinicians from a day earlier as they began their routines exactly where they had left off the night before. I was now beginning to sense a problem and that I may be in worse condition than we all thought. By ten o'clock that morning, my wife arrived back at the hospital after taking the kids to school and pulling the strict Mommy duties that were demanded of her. She sat down, and we began chatting about the kids' morning, my brutal night, and the surgery.

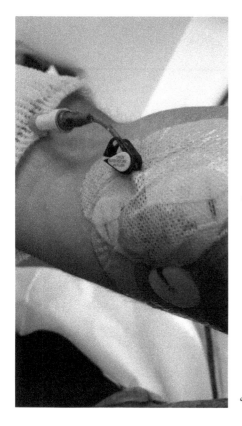

Then a knock at the door, followed by four doctors. It was my surgeon, the infectious disease doctor, and two other doctors that were tagging along. I was asked if I had been out of the country over the last thirty days or had any cuts or scrapes on my body. The answers were all no. The surgeon then said, "Brian, we encountered some problems yesterday with your surgery. Your spine was extremely inflamed and was in unbelievably bad shape. Your spinal bone looked as if it were moth-eaten and could have caused you to be paralyzed." He went on to say that he ordered a multitude of tests "to find out what happened to you and to eliminate any further assumptions we may have had." And just like that, they said, "At first glimpse we thought you had an aggressive form of bone cancer; however, through further studies, procedures, and testing we have diagnosed you with a bone-eating staphylococcus infection."

This serious infection was attached to my spine and was eating away at the spinal bone, disc, and tissue of my spine. It was also doing a slew of damage inside my belly where my bladder was now dramatically impacted by this near-fatal infection, and later you will find out the further damage that was later detected and diagnosed as a direct result of this spinal infection.

The doctors were stunned that this infection went on for so long, and at times even saying I was incredibly lucky to be alive given the potent nature of the infection, how long it was in my body, and where it was in relation to my spinal cord, nerves, and so on, also relaying that sepsis could have easily set in and killed me within days.

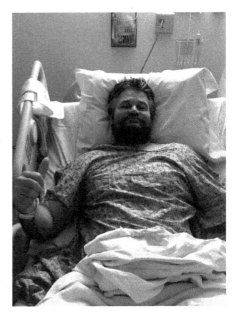

They delivered this scary news, ordered a PICC line in which IV antibiotics would be administered three times a day for the next three months, and abruptly left the room. That was a lot of information for me to take in as I felt worried, scared, and defeated. With my wife by my side, we shared a long hug and she promised everything would be okay.

The good news was I did not have cancer, so that was the most important thing in our eyes; however, having a diagnosis of a bone-eating staph infection that destroyed the innards of my body was not a walk in the park either. After spending a week in the hospital, I was finally released and sent home. I knew I had a rough road ahead of me; however I was thrilled to be going home.

As you will come to find out, this was just the onset of an enormous snowball effect that was just beginning to have an enormous impact on my life and the life of my family for years and years to come.

CHAPTER 8:
REST, RECOVERY, AND REALIZATION

After I got home, I was still in a lot of pain and tremendous discomfort. I was limited to my room and my chair where I felt the most comfort and relief. My wife was an absolute angel of mine and took care of me better than I could take care of myself. She is and was the true embodiment of a Marine wife and lived by the words *Semper Fi*, which means "always faithful." She waited on me hand and foot, administering IV antibiotics every four hours, making my meals, washing me, helping me in the bathroom, and further assisting me with all the activities of daily living.

Brian and Jenny just months before his malpractice incident

She was the best caretaker anyone could ever have, and she truly demonstrated the marital promise of "till death do us part." I am incredibly lucky to have her. As the days turned into weeks, weeks into months, and months into years, I wasn't improving physically, and by now I was absolutely shot mentally and emotionally. All I wanted was to get better and pick up where I left off prior to becoming sick.

At this point I just wanted to get back to work, provide for my family once again, and recapture some sort of normalcy.

Our community and friends came together to help my family and me with meal trains, and some folks graciously helped us monetarily with paying a few bills during this time of uncertainty. We were absolutely blown away by the empathy and compassion that was displayed to my family and me. These meals helped keep my wife and children fed without my wife being taken away from caring for me. She was able to concentrate all her attention on my needs, and she did not have to worry about shopping and making meals.

The meal deliveries, combined with our friends taking our kids to their respective sporting events and extracurricular actives, definitely helped the kids maintain their sense of normalcy despite nothing being normal around them. The gratitude that my family and I have toward everyone that helped us in our most desperate and trying times is something I cannot explain or even put into words.

As a father I could not have been prouder of my children for answering their very own call to service and stepping up around the house, caring for me, helping Mom, and never veering off course.

Their schoolwork, sports and activity schedules, along with their responsibilities were never affected by what was happening. My wife played a monumental role in ensuring that this moment in time would not be taken away from them and we wanted nothing more than having our children enjoy their childhood and live their best lives through this unknown process.

Of course, my kids worried about me, but my wife and their

coaches, teachers, and friends helped keep their minds positive and focused on everything that was beautiful around us rather than the negatives that were surrounding us. All my children wanted was a sense of normalcy again and to spend time with the whole family again.

One of the hardest things about what happened is I had never missed any of my kids' games in my life, and it killed me to have missed so much. I do vaguely remember getting out on a few occasions, because I could not stand missing them play. I took my meds, and my wife loaded up my walker and we made our way to the ball fields and made the absolute best of it. I had to get in a few games, even when I was

on my deathbed, and when I came out to support the kiddos, they always played extra hard to earn the game ball, in which they tossed to me after the game. I watched on as I lived through some proud moments, and many beautiful memories were made that I will cherish for the rest of my life. Nothing has ever made me so proud of the resilience of my family!

During my toughest times, it killed me to not be able to just play catch with my kids. My little guy Colton begged me to go out with him one day, and despite the tough recovery process and pain, I did. He said, "Dad, all you have to do is watch," as my children thrived for my attention and had missed their dad. I brought my chair out to the field and I watched my kids play catch. It had been quite some time since I last experienced a moment such as the one, I was currently living in. Colton even carried the base-ball equipment, and he would not even let me touch it.

The smells of the fresh-cut grass, jasmine, and magnolia filled the air with joy, and I felt at peace. It had been an awfully long time since I had gotten out and enjoyed the finer things in my life and had been so thankful for my beautiful and loving family. I was a man full of gratitude.

My children all remained fully involved and engaged in school and all their extracurricular activities, despite the horrifying hardship we were living through as a family. You can see that, through it all, my kids excelled and were very well taken care of. My wife deserves all the credit in the world as she was the glue that kept everything together. Every now and then I would take a peek out the window and would sometimes see the little ones doing homework together while enjoying

a nice afternoon outside on a sunny Southern California day. What a blessing!

(Photo prior to injury and malpractice incident)

One thing about my family is that we have always been each other's biggest fans and supporters. We never do anything without all of us in attendance. We are truly an inseparable family. During these times of trial and tribulation, my family remained unscathed and unscratched. My family is as solid as a rock, and we all were praying and hoping that the storm we were in would soon come to an end.

Unfortunately, the pain was too much to bear at times and severely limited my ability to be who I once was. My life became consumed with never-ending doctor's appointments, medical procedures, additional surgeries, counseling, and physical therapy. I struggled mightily with self-identity and purpose, and I lost all my confidence as I began to slip further and further away from the reality I faced.

My severe physical pain led to severe anxiety, and the anxiety led to depression, and the depression led to self-isolation. They all feed off each other and having all three working in unison at the same time was

absolute hell. I completely gave up on myself and sat in my chair, in my room, battled alone, and separated myself from the world, completely tuning everything out as my life fell apart.

One of the hardest parts thus far in this journey was the constant worry and fear that I was going to lose everything I had ever worked so hard for in my life because of this horrible medical malpractice experience and becoming injured due to no fault of my own.

Months went on and medical treatment continued. It literally has never ended. The smells of hospitals and clinics make me sick, and the smells of antibiotics

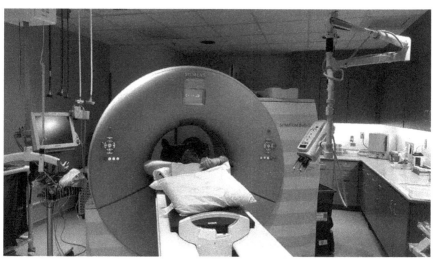

being injected into me, along with the saline smell and alcohol swabs, to this day make me ill. The never-ending procedures, blood draws, and dressing changes were all a new part of life, and essential for my survival. I was injured at thirty-eight years old, and I am now forty-four, and the endless doctors' appointments and quarterly checkups will be something I will have to do for the rest of my life.

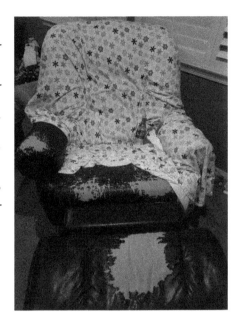

My life was my chair, my meds, and the four walls I stared at, shaking my head as I felt so hopeless and helpless with no way out. I did so because I did not want to burden anyone. That meant pushing some of my dearest friends in the world away because the happy-go-lucky, positive, energetic, and fun-loving guy that I once had been was no longer the same man that they had grown to love and appreciate. The last thing I ever wanted to do is bring others down and have them listen to my medical problems, my financial woes, and a grown man feeling sorry for himself.

Our savings account began to dwindle, credit card debt went through the roof, and we began losing things such as my small business, tools, equipment, and our family car, as well as my self-worth and identity on who I was as a man, father, and husband. It was absolutely killing me. Keep in mind I never even had a late payment on anything in my life, let alone a credit card. Prior to this incident, I had perfect credit and was now sinking further into debt while my wife did everything she could to stave off utter collapse.

I was now one year into this nightmare with no source of income, loss of earnings, and loss of future earnings. I had no other option than to file a tort claim against the VA for medical malpractice and gross negligence causing permanent injury and nearly death. To this point, my family and I had been through hell, and I began to fully understand just what the clear definition of "pain and suffering" truly was, and it was not pretty.

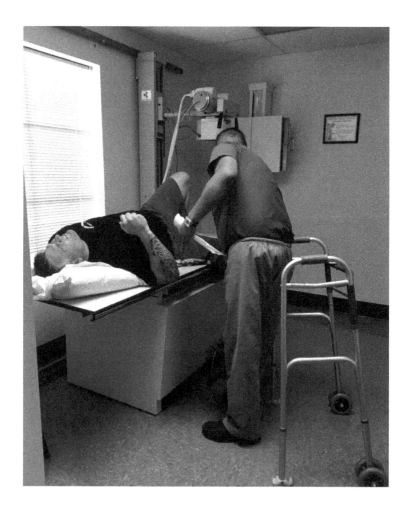

CHAPTER 9:
FILING THE FTCA TORT CLAIM SF 95

In March 2017 I found out through a myelogram that this untreated and near-fatal infection caused permanent injuries and damage to all three levels of my spine, my bladder, and kidney renal function, plus neuropathy (severe nerve damage) and countless of other medical issues relating to my four-month-long bone-eating staph infection that aggressively ate my spine. It ultimately led to a host of other residual

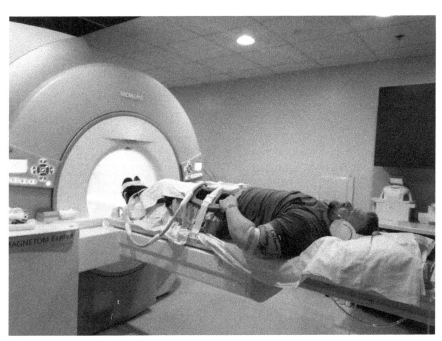

medical diagnoses, which in turn led my family and me to file a claim under the Federal Tort Claims Act (FTCA) for medical malpractice and gross negligence.

The first thing I did was contact the patient advocate at the VA hospital, and they referred me to the hospital leadership and the director's office. They gave me the SF 95 to fill out and send off to the regional General Counsel's office in Los Angeles. I was told that my tort claim would be completed in six months and to look for an answer by October 2017.

I immediately began to call attorneys from around the country to assist me with my claim. This was yet another roadblock and unfortunate experience in front of me: explaining my case and story to the "call screeners" while my cognitive function was completely out of whack due to the endless number of pills I was still taking. I had a ridiculously hard time speaking and communicating effectively. So, I started to write and send emails instead. Every single attorney I reached out to said my case was egregious and that I had a case vs. the VA; however, they all declined to take my case solely based on the, and I quote, "red tape bureaucratic process of the VA, and the handling of the tort claims process."

These attorneys otherwise stated that if this would have happened in a civilian hospital, they would immediately represent me. The VA makes it so difficult for these attorneys to represent injured veterans after they have already been put on their knees due to no fault of their own and essentially left with no counsel. Why would an attorney take these VA government cases when they know the amount of work that would need to be done is probably five times that of a civilian case?

Meanwhile my ongoing medical treatment never let up. My wife continued to not only be my caregiver, but she also became my full-time taxi driver. I had appointments nearly every other day, and up to this point, my life was consumed with endless doctor's appointments. They consisted of monthly blood tests to check for the infection, continued physical therapy, pain management, urology, orthopedic surgeons, infectious disease doctors, MRIs, x-rays, and mental health care.

It was extremely difficult to juggle all of this on my own, but it was a necessary reality. The infection did so much damage to all three levels

of my spine and internal organs, and we were just beginning to find out the full extent of the permanent injury my body endured. Just imagine for a moment being eaten alive for one day and the damage it could do. Well, now imagine that for four months. The damage was significant, but I was a man that was full of gratitude to be alive and a man that was also grieving as a part of me had died.

After sixteen denials in two months from attorneys, I began to fight this and advocate my case on my own. I wrote out a timeline and backed it all up with factual medical evidence, compiled all of my medical records, and mailed this all to the regional General Counsel's office as further evidence for the tort claim that I previously had mailed out and filed in March as it was now nearing June 2017.

My family and I waited patiently for the six-month mark to roll around, and when it did, I immediately made a call and contacted the VA attorney that was reviewing my tort claim and case. I wanted to be as proactive as possible. The VA attorney stated to me that a decision had not been made yet on my case and that it had been sent out of my region and on to the southeast region due to "realignment" among the Office of General Counsel. Soon thereafter I began to receive calls from the VA General Counsel's office in North Carolina.

The attorney that was assigned my case made several calls, and she stated repeatedly, and I quote, "The VA failed to meet the standard of care, and there was a breach in liability, and we are looking to settle your claim." We were asked to be patient as "this is a very long and tiring process." The VA attorney appeared very sincere and apologetic and showed a great deal of compassion. We were now being led down a garden path full of hope, as some of our worries and anxieties began to slowly ease up.

These optimistic calls also came at our most desperate and vulnerable times of need, and they continued for several months. We were able to breathe a sigh of relief, knowing that we could potentially stave off complete financial ruin and begin to focus our attention solely on my health. Then nearly at the one-year mark of filing my tort claim, the bombshell dropped, and my world, and that of my family, was turned upside down and was undeniably crushed, as we were left holding the bag in a state of hopelessness, helplessness, and nowhere to turn.

CHAPTER 10:
THE TECHNICALITY AND THE DENIAL

On a letter dated November 1, 2017, and postmarked weeks later, and received just days before Thanksgiving, we received a response from the VA's Office of General Counsel. The VA had dropped a bombshell on my family and me, and the letter stated that the VA was no longer responsible for the substandard care I received because of a law that was written in 1946 that said the United States is not liable for claims arising from the acts of an independent contractor. Simply put, contractors are not federal agencies, and their employees are not "employees of the Government" such that the United States would be liable for any tortious acts or omissions by the contractor. What is the Federal Tort Claims Act? Since its enactment in 1946, the Federal Torts Claims Act (FTCA) has been the legal mechanism for compensating people who have suffered personal injury by the negligent or wrongful action of employees of the US government. The FTCA permits an individual to bring a lawsuit directly against the federal government for certain VA-caused injury or death, when that individual has suffered damages, personal injury, or death due to the negligent actions of a federal government employee or agency acting within the scope of employment.

Federal law determines who is an "employee" vs. "independent contractor," but the scope of employment issues under the FTCA is decided by the state law of occurrence. The FTCA defines "employee of the government" to include "officers or employees of any federal agency…

and persons acting on behalf of a federal agency in an official capacity, temporarily or permanently in the service of the United States." Many VA hospitals and facilities currently hire independent contractors to perform medical procedures and provide health care. These individuals are not considered government employees; therefore, any malpractice claims will not give rise to a claim under the FTCA. The government often denies liability and contends that the alleged negligence was not caused by an employee but an independent contractor. This legal defense is highly effective unless dealt with adequately, as VA medical centers frequently contract with private universities or hospitals for physicians. In each situation, the Office of General Counsel must isolate the portion of work out of which the claim arose. If an employer-employee relationship is present, the government is held liable. If the injury was caused by an independent contractor, the government is not liable. The independent contractor can still be sued in their private capacities in state court but not under the FTCA.

The FTCA's definition of "government employee" includes officers and employees of federal agencies, but specifically excludes "any contractor with the United States" (28 U.S.C. § 2671). Thus, the independent contractor exception to the FTCA often bars federal government liability and denies FTCA protection to the defendant party. The independent contractor is thereby liable for damages as a private citizen.

I will now describe, through my experience, how this law is ruining the lives of veterans because it has turned into a "legal loophole" and is no longer working in the way it was intended to work since its creation in 1946. A lot has changed over the last seventy-four years pertaining to independent contractors working within VA hospitals and clinics across the country. This is why immediate legislative correction was needed without further delay to ensure the rights and protections of all veterans.

Now that you understand how the contractor exception works, let me reiterate what had just happened here. In late November 2017, we received a letter from the VA's Office of General Counsel. The letter stated that the VA was no longer responsible for the substandard care

I received because of a law that was written in 1946 that states the US government is not responsible for "non"-US government employees.

So, the VA reversed course, did an about-face, denied my claim based on a technicality and an employment status, and left me and my family holding the bag—even though the VA acknowledged the wrongdoing repeatedly, and even admitted it through media publications through their public affairs spokesperson.

They also stated to me in the letter that I would have to sue the independent contractor in state court to hold her accountable for her actions. The letter was postmarked just mere days after my California state statute of limitations had expired, leaving me and my family with no viable recourse, accountability, or justice.

So now my life was not only being destroyed due to medical malpractice and gross negligence but was now being dealt yet another blow, having to deal with legal malpractice and unfair, unjust, and fraudulent actions from the highest levels of the Department of Veterans Affairs. The VA essentially watched the clock on my case and led my family and me down that garden path of hope, and once they were in the clear, they dropped the letter. This tactic has also proved to be beneficial to the VA to protect their independent contractors as well.

Once that state statute of limitation expires, the clinician cannot even be reported to the National Practitioner Data Bank. By doing so, the VA does not have any independent contract clinicians with bad paper, or complaints, and they have gone unreported. This also works very well to water down the actual medical malpractice cases that happen in the VA annually. The VA attorneys were so apologetic and were absolutely engaged in my case to the point where I thought that everything that needed to be done was being done. This news absolutely crushed us, knowing now that the VA had effectively stripped me of my right to due process not only in state court but also in federal court.

They blamed it all on an independent contractor who was working within the halls and the walls of the VA hospital. Even though the VA found several other clinicians who were indeed VA employees and were also guilty of failing to meet the standard of care, they placed the blame solely on the back of the independent contractor. The VA did this to see their way out of paying rightful compensation for hurting me due to no fault of my own.

So essentially, they were able to legally deflect all liability away from the VA and place it solely on the back of an unidentified independent contractor that was working within the halls and the walls of the VA. Unfortunately, many veterans, if not all, have no idea that their clinicians are more than likely independent contractors. They have VA business cards, VA doctors' coats, they see VA patients, use VA supplies, and in most cases even have keys to the building. In some cases, these so-called independent contractors would be labeled as "employees"; however, in the case of the VA, they are independent.

This scheme has been widely used and has been quite effective for the VA to avoid paying out rightful medical malpractice settlements. In my eyes this was not only fraudulent but criminal, and I knew something needed to be done to stop this injustice and put an end to this egregious seventy-four-year VA legal loophole that has destroyed the lives of veterans and their families for generations.

Just when you thought things could not get any stranger, the next chapter will leave you saying to yourself, "You can't make this stuff up." Soon we will be faced with an ultimatum out of nowhere and will be strong-armed into accepting a "litigation risk" settlement.

It was too late for my family and me to have justice, accountability, transparency, and legal recourse due to a seventy-four-year VA legal loophole, but it was not too late to protect the rest of the veteran population estimated at 20.2 million American veterans and the 9 million American veterans currently enrolled within the VA system.

This egregious loophole is criminal and has dishonored veterans and their families at their lowest and most vulnerable and desperate times in need! This can never happen again.

CHAPTER 11:

THE VA COVER-UP, LIES, AND STRONG-ARM BACKROOM DEAL

IN THIS CHAPTER I WILL EXPLAIN IN GREAT DETAIL AND TRY TO WALK YOU down this entire tort claims process. I ended up filing a second tort claim for the legal malpractice that happened when the VA initially denied my tort claim based on the employment status and technicality that I explained in the last chapter.

I never had an opportunity to see a judge in federal court because the Office of General Counsel stated that my case would never go to court based on the "independent contractor exception law." This is how the loophole is beginning to take shape, as you can clearly see, by protecting the VA and its independent contractors while running the clock on injured veterans and effectively stripping veterans of their right to due process. Just imagine for a moment your life changing due to no fault of your own, and now you have been stripped of your right to due process and have no legal recourse or justice. Is this America? Is this how we treat our nations veterans?

I was not given an opportunity to tell my story to a federal judge or a state judge, and essentially my rights were stripped of me in a time of extreme vulnerability to include emotional, mental, and physical pain. I had questions that were never answered as well as some facts about my story, including doctor's reports and reasoning behind my serious accusations.

In my opinion and also based solely on facts and documented reports, findings, and official correspondence, I believe the VA acted in ways that were obviously unethical and malicious from the very beginning. I believe the VA intended on using this legal loophole against my family and me. The VA also knew I did not have legal representation because I could not find an attorney to take my case, so they took advantage of my vulnerability and saw the perfect storm to put the dagger through our hearts and essentially finish us off.

In March 2017 I filed my initial tort claim with the VA due to gross neglect and medical malpractice causing permanent injury and nearly death in the amount of $2,175,000. The typical turnaround time for a tort claim is said to be at or around six months. In September 2017, a VA attorney conducted a phone interview with me. She had concluded that the "VA failed to meet the standard of care, and there was a breach in liability." She then explained to me to remain patient as a settlement was coming my way, and these cases take time to sort out.

The good news was that the VA had openly admitted the fault and that the negligence and malpractice did indeed take place. This took some much-needed stress off the family, knowing that a settlement was coming our way. Again, the VA attorney was extremely apologetic and apologized over again that they were sorry that I received substandard care and that the clinicians failed to meet the standard of care.

In November 2017 I was informed that my primary care physician at the time of neglect and malpractice was not a VA employee but rather an "independent contractor," so therefore the VA was not accountable or responsible under FTCA law. I was then informed I had to seek legal damages with the doctor through state court. The letter also stated they would continue investigating the extent of liability by other clinicians that were involved in my care as I was seen twice in the VA emergency room prior to seeing my primary care physician.

The amount of time it took the VA to properly inform me of this "technicality" and employment status was nearly one year. This was all critical information that should have been rightfully given to me right out of the gate and immediately after filing my tort claim. It should have been the first box that was checked during the initial intake by the VA Office of General Counsel.

Because of this delay, the VA effectively blew my chances of filing suit in the state of California because my state statute of limitations had expired by mere days. I was now left with zero accountability, recourse, or justice, and the independent contractor was left with zero repercussions and maintained a clean record and remained in good standing as a VA clinician.

In January 2018 I received a flat-out denial by the VA, stating that the VA emergency room met the standard of care and there was zero liability on their part, which was extremely confusing, because by this point, I had already been told on dozens of occasions that the "VA failed to meet the standard of care."

Once the VA found out an independent contractor was involved in my care, they placed all liability on my primary care physician, stepped back, did an about-face, wiped their hands clean, and denied my claim based on an employment status. I immediately filed a request for reconsideration.

In February 2018 my brother, Scott, was absolutely blown away at what had taken place thus far and was dumbfounded on these conclusions and how manipulative the VA was. He had enough, and he began to advocate on my behalf as my cognitive state was having a negative impact on my thinking and speaking. The powerful narcotics, mixed in with this emotional roller coaster, was having a taxing effect on my body, and I could not do this any longer on my own.

My brother began reaching out to anyone that would listen, because he felt this was a downright travesty. It seemed as if my life as I knew it was over, all due to no fault of my own. My depression, anxiety, and physical pain began to spiral out of control, and I remained in my chair, self-isolating and doing everything I could to separate myself from life, as I was mentally and emotionally checked out. As my brother began to dig, send letters, and make dozens of calls, he reached out to different VA hospitals, trying to seek as much knowledge as he possibly could about their processes and procedures. Within a month he started to receive some solid information on how we could possibly proceed, and it came from VA hospital leadership from across the country.

On February 21, 2018, I filed an 1151 claim, which was recommended by a local VA director. An 1151 claim is a malpractice claim that is filed "in house" and is completed through the VA rating department. The 1151 claims are filed for compensation due to the injury or death proximately caused by "carelessness, negligence, lack of proper skill, error in judgment, or similar instance of fault" or by "an event not reasonably foreseeable" in VA's furnishing of hospital care, medical treatment, surgical treatment, or examination. In short, Section 1151 claims only involve injury or death due to the administering of medical care, as opposed to incidents that might occur on a VA facility campus.

If a Section 1151 claim is resolved in favor of the claimant, the injury or death is considered as if it were a service-connected disability. This means that the injury or condition will be rated according to the VA rating schedule and will be compensated accordingly on a monthly basis. Shortly after filing my 1151 claim, I received my medical examination, which was done outside of the VA and performed under an independent review. The doctors conducted a thorough independent examination that included a wide variety of tests and completed an independent review of my records. These appointments took several weeks to complete, and once everything was submitted back to the VA is when the next stage of waiting began.

On May 2, 2018, the chief counsel from the VA Office of General Counsel began to communicate with me via email. He stated that he was working on my request for reconsideration from my original tort claim denial. He also wanted to know the outcome of my 1151 that I had just filed, as I believe he was making his decision based solely on that independent review and outcome. Shortly thereafter, within a week of my initial contact with the chief counsel from the VA's headquarters in Washington, DC, I was informed that my 1151 was abruptly and flat-out denied.

The reasoning for their denial was that my case did not have any evidence of "carelessness, negligence, lack of proper skill, error in judgment, or similar instance of fault on the part of the Department." They go on to say that "merely showing that a veteran has additional disability is not sufficient to establish causation." Entitlement to compensation under 38 U.S.C. § 1151 for lumbar pain with staph infection *denied*.

Yet another letdown in my sea of ongoing denials and deflection. So now I had a denied federal tort claim and a denied 1151 after being told by numerous VA attorneys that the VA failed to meet the standard of care and a settlement was coming my way. I immediately filed my appeal and reached out to the chief counsel for explanation.

On May 29, 2018, the VA and the chief counsel must have had information leaked to them regarding my case because at that time I was offered a $50,000 settlement directly from the chief counsel, and it was offered over a telephone call. The chief counsel cleverly called the settlement a "litigation risk," and under no circumstances could they fairly compensate me in full due to the FTCA contractor exception law. This is the moment where I believe the chief counsel knew that I had a case vs. the VA emergency room staff, who were VA employees, and he made an exceptionally low offer to me, knowing that this information would soon surface, to essentially save the VA from paying out a two-million-dollar medical malpractice claim.

On June 6, 2018, I retained legal counsel. It was quite easy to find a lawyer now that there was essentially blood in the water, now that a VA offer had been made. My attorney and the chief counsel negotiated the litigation risk to a total of $150K, netting me a total of $125K, after I paid my attorney the other $25K. As I questioned my attorney, I asked over and over again, how could the VA legally offer me any money after they already stated that they legally could not compensate veterans that were harmed by non-US government employees? I literally could not keep up or even comprehend what was happening.

None of this made sense. I told my attorney that this was not an acceptable offer and the amount I was respectfully asking for was $2,175,000, not $150,000. By the middle of June 2018, I was informed that this was my final offer. It was a take-it-or-leave-it moment for me. I was advised by my attorney that I would be left with zero if I did not accept this final offer. You read that right, *zero*, nothing!

The chief counsel told my attorney that it would never get to federal court, and if it did, it would be immediately thrown out of court due to the contractor exception law. That was the defense of the VA, and I was told it was very strong, as this law from 1946 was undeniably bulletproof.

On June 28, 2018, after being backed into a corner and literally strong-armed, at the lowest point in my life and the highest moment of vulnerability, I accepted the litigation risk of $125K as I was in the midst of losing my home after not working for well over two years due to my permanent injury caused by gross neglect and malpractice, due to no fault of my own.

My family and I had already lost enough, and we could not afford to lose anything else. If I had not accepted this offer, cleverly packaged as "litigation risk," I was told that the chief counsel would have just given me a second denial and I would be left with zero, so obviously I had to take it. I did not have a choice.

Within two weeks of signing the "litigation risk" for $150K, $25K of that going directly to my attorney, I received a letter in the mail from the VA. It was the 1151 appeal that was originally denied and was now approved at the 100 percent level to include special monthly compensation due to the gross neglect and malpractice, which resulted in just a $100 increase in disability payments per month. I was absolutely mind blown and flabbergasted how this was all unfolding. Nothing was adding up, and something definitely wasn't passing the smell test.

To my surprise while reading the decision and doctor's report, not only was my primary care physician responsible for my gross neglect and malpractice, but the VA emergency room staff was also responsible for not properly triaging me, not once but twice with the signs and symptoms I posed. This damning report went on to say that delayed and denied care and neglectful actions "allowed for further destruction of the spinal column." The medical reviewer refers to Brian's "permanent injury" and the "red flags" missed by health care providers at the VA.

He also believed the injury to the spinal cord "also led to the veteran's current lumbar IVDS, erectile dysfunction and bladder paralysis," just to name a few of the serious permanent conditions that I now live with. The report also stated the infection should have been caught from the onset by a simple blood test. A diagnosis of the infection early on would have been treated with oral antibiotics and would have prevented much of the disability from the lumbar spine infection. This report effectively proves my case and furthermore solidifies what was being told to me repeatedly from the very beginning, and that is that the "VA failed to meet the standard of care, and there was a breach in liability."

I found this rather convenient, and suspicious, on the VA's part to have denied me over and over again as I stacked denial on top of denial. Then out of nowhere I get backed into a corner of vulnerability. Force me into an extremely low settlement amount, and effectively deny my right to a fair trial or even see a judge. Then approve my appeal of the 1151 that was just completely denied and then gets approved with a fully favorable decision of 100 percent, to also include special monthly compensation for an internal loss of an organ. Ultimately what happened here is the VA saved the two million dollars in the lawsuit by denying and deflecting all responsibility and accountability and turned right around and accepted responsibility and accountability. In a written statement, the VA said it "always strives to provide Veterans with the very best health care available. When we don't meet that standard, we hold ourselves accountable. In this case, we worked with the Veteran and his attorney in an effort to avoid litigation and settled this unfortunate case in a way we hope is meaningful to Mr. Tally."

After I read that statement the VA put out, it made me nauseous and physically sick. The blatant lies, corruption, and fraudulent actions that were being orchestrated at the highest levels of the Department of Veterans Affairs were not only scary but downright frightening. All I could think to myself is how can these guys get away with this. It was absolutely crazy, and I just sat in shock and amazement, thinking to myself, "You can't make this stuff up."

I knew something needed to be done to put an end to this heinous act. If I was going to be the man to shine a light on this systemic and unfair practice, and essentially expose made men, successful men, with high-profile jobs within the US Government, I would need to look at myself in the mirror, make a decision, and ask myself, is this something worth fighting for?

It took a ton of thinking on what decision I would make and begin this fight in Congress and tell my story in an effort to spark a conversation and ultimately change federal law to give all veterans the rights and protections they deserve. I was afraid and nervous. I had a family, and I was told that guys sometimes end up dead for exposing these types of practices in high level government positions. I did not want to end up dead or have any problems, and I made that point clear. It did freak me out, I am not going to lie. Perhaps it could have been a mix of my severe anxiety and worry combined with folks that watch way too many movies.

Regardless, the loophole was just so bad, and my family and I experienced so much hardship, including a mental and emotional toll on our bodies. As I began uncovering jaw-dropping information on how these cases were manipulated by VA attorneys, I embarked on a mission to change the very law that essentially ruined my life. I decided that it was important enough to build up the courage I needed to stand up, and give the voiceless a voice, and fight for what's right, and do it all for the "good of the country," and protect the lives of all veterans. Therefore, all veterans rallied around the "Tally Bill" to ensure the rights and protections of all veterans. You never know, it could be you, a family member, a friend, or even your neighbor that will be affected next.

This was no longer about me or my story. It was bigger than that. I could have also completely cut my losses and forgotten about everything and lived a life of, "I should have tried to change the law" or "I could have done something." I did not want to become a bitter man that did nothing but sit back and complain about how horrible a situation my family fell into. I simply wanted to turn a negative into a positive and wanted to move forward in a way that was sincere, professional, and positive. I was not interested in name calling, name dropping, slandering any organization, or causing any unnecessary issues or drama. I just wanted to ensure the rights and protections of all veterans and create a clear path of legal recourse to those injured veterans that have already nearly lost it all- including assets, livelihoods, and their physical, mental, and emotional health, all due to no fault of their own.

This famous quote from former President John F. Kennedy motivated me to never quit, and never give up, despite the enormous uphill battle I faced; "Ask not what your country can do for you, but what you can do for your country"

CHAPTER 12:

CONGRESSIONAL INVESTIGATION, LOTS OF QUESTIONS, AND NO ANSWERS!

DESPERATELY REACHED OUT TO MY CONGRESSMAN IN DIRE NEED, TO appeal this decision that had just been handed down to me. I lived in the 50th district in California, and my representative was Duncan Hunter, who was also a former Marine and the son of longtime congressman Duncan Hunter Sr.

At first, he was immediately engaged and wrote several letters to the Office of General Counsel. In his first letter, he asked that an investigation be conducted into my case and case findings. He went on to say that the Office of General Counsel did not adequately address what seems to be systematic problems within the VA tort claims process. Representative Duncan Hunter requested a personal review of the situation and to provide him with solutions that not only will assist me but will also avoid other U.S. veterans from becoming victims of the same situation.

It was in the second letter that Congressman Duncan Hunter got a bit fiery, asked some tough questions, and began to demand the answers we were looking for. Here is the congressman in his own words:

> Apparently, VA contracted employees employed at VA facilities are not subject to malpractice tort claims. However, the tort denial notification process and response time is

lacking the necessary safeguards to protect our veterans from the bureaucratic "red tape" of this policy. Even more troubling is that the Office of General Counsel acknowledged, with no apparent concern, that Mr. Tally's tort eligibility determination process took nearly a year. That excessively long period of time put him beyond the state of California's statute of limitations to file a medical malpractice claim, thus leaving him with no legal recourse for the poor care he received at the VA Loma Linda Healthcare System. This is completely unacceptable.

Signed, Duncan Hunter—Member of Congress

Here is a list of questions that were asked by Representative Duncan Hunter as to why I fell through the cracks and how the VA can deny this rightful tort claim. This correspondence went on for several months as we were repeatedly ignored by the Office of General Counsel as they failed to answer the simple questions my congressman asked.

1. Why was Mr. Tally not notified sooner, and given the employment status of the accused clinician?
2. What was the basis for the change in the legal finding by the Office of General Counsel of ineligibility to file a tort claim?
3. Is there currently a requirement or directive for the VA to provide accountability for contract employees providing health treatment in terms of reporting violations to appropriate medical licensing boards?

Below is the reply, or lack thereof, by the Office of General Counsel in Washington, DC, in the words from the chief counsel. "Mr. Tally's claim was investigated but denied by letter dated January 17th, 2018. The investigation included determining whether the involved medical providers were Government employees. Under the Federal Tort Claims Act (FTCA). The Government may only be liable for acts and/or omissions of its employees." He went on to add that the fact that one provider was an independent contractor did not preclude the VA from thoroughly investigating the claim to determine whether other providers might have been negligent in the care provided.

My congressman and I both found this response tasteless and incorrect. In my opinion they knew immediately who was responsible for the malpractice by simply pulling my chart and viewing the clinicians involved in my care. It seemed as if the Office of General Counsel had already strategized this outcome and was able to cherry-pick the clinicians involved in my care by screening everyone involved and was able to tie at least one independent contractor to my case and preselected the "fall guy" based on the independent contractor clause and exemption. This is how the VA Office of General Counsel gained the upper hand. They repeatedly fed my family and me false hope and promises only to pull the rug right out from under our feet, denying our claim based on a "technicality" and an employment status, and left us holding the bag with no viable recourse, accountability, or due process.

During the heat of my ongoing battle with the VA's Office of General Counsel, the only hope my family and I had left was my congressman and the voice we had in Washington. No sooner did we begin to gain some positive traction in my case, Representative Duncan Hunter landed himself in a bit of trouble. It was a significant blow and nearly the knockout punch to my mission and cause. We were on a solid path of exposing this egregious loophole and fraudulent practices that were being orchestrated by the highest levels of the Department of Veterans Affairs, and now I found myself with no Congressman.

On August 21, 2018, a federal grand jury of the United States District Court for the Southern District of California indicted Representative Duncan Hunter and his wife on sixty counts of wire fraud, falsifying records, campaign finance violations, and conspiracy. He was then stripped of his congressional committees and any credibility he had left, as his days in Congress were now essentially over. From this moment forward, he and his office staff became irrelevant and completely disengaged from continuing to help me with my case and ended up ignoring our repeated requests for help during the toughest and most vulnerable times of me and my family's life. It was a significant punch to the gut.

In a last-ditch effort, I fired off a letter solely out of anger and frustration, hoping he could at least order a full-fledged investigation prior to completely leaving Congress. The letter was received by Representative Hunter's chief of staff, but his office never followed up with me.

It was yet another obstacle, a brick wall if you will, that stood in my way, and it even came with an "out." I had every reason from this point to quit, walk away, try to pick up the pieces of my life that lay shattered about, and do everything in our power to try and stay afloat through this wicked storm that we found ourselves in. Some time went on, and my anxiety and depression began to compound like interest and spiraled out of control as everything around me began to unravel.

My hopes, dreams, aspirations and my life as I once knew it was over. The fear of losing everything and the realization that my family and I had literally been destroyed by the hands of the very government that it vows to protect were disheartening, as hopelessness, helplessness, and defeat filled my soul. I remember a day in mid-2018 when everything continued to fall apart around me while I was laid up in a chair in my room where I spent my days, self-isolating and escaping the harsh reality of life and pain.

I began to cry and sob, and as my wife came in to check on me, I told her, "How can this happen to good people and good families?" Something has got to be done about this egregious loophole, and we need to fix it. I was tired, exhausted, and defeated beyond anything you could imagine. I was 99 percent done, at the verge of giving up, but something in me told me to keep fighting. At that time, I just stood up and walked to my bathroom, took my medication, and kneeled over my bathtub.

I was crying uncontrollably, and I filled that tub up with my tears. It was at this point I let everything out, and I cried out to God, and prayed. I explained I did not have much left to give, but I had 1 percent left in me. I repeatedly asked God to give me the courage, commitment, endurance, and strength I would need and to guide me on this painstaking journey and mission that I knew would be extremely difficult, painful, and full of fear and anxiety.

I was so scared, and I had never been afraid of anything before in my life, but this scenario I was now in had literally put me on my knees, and it had kept me there for years, and it was time to stand up, prepare, strategize, and pray to my heavenly Father to equip me with everything I would need, every tool possible, to see that this extremely important mission was accomplished. I prayed that one day we would soon realize that transparency, recourse, and justice would be effectively put in place, and we would restore some much-needed faith and confidence within the VA medical system. I opened my heart, showed my vulnerability, and once again, accepted and answered the call to service and country.

I promised myself that night before God that I would change the very law that ruined my life and the thousands of others that came before me. I would hold myself accountable to that very promise by starting a Facebook page called "Rally Around Tally," where I would lay out my daily tasks, and agenda on what I was doing each day to fight for all veterans, change a generational loophole, create legislation, and make a positive impact. I held myself accountable to that very promise and used it as a tool and motivation to keep me laser focused and dead set on the mission and task at hand. It was the starting point and acknowledgement I needed to begin this next chapter in my life and set sail on a mission to protect my fellow veterans.

CHAPTER 13:

NO CONGRESSMAN, NO PROBLEM— BECOMING THE VOICE OF CHANGE

SAT IN MY CHAIR, FUMBLING WITH MY PHONE AND A PAD OF PAPER. Googling, researching, and scratching my head over what I needed to do to bring about real positive change and veteran reform within the VA. Most veterans understand it is exceedingly difficult to just schedule an appointment or to simply even have a phone call answered within a reasonable amount of time without spending hours on hold. So needless to say, this was going to be quite the learning process for me, having never been formally trained in advocacy, lobbying, or communicating with elected officials. By this time, it had been just over two and a half years since my injury, and I had not worked since.

The only thing I had was a newfound purpose, some passion, and a plan. I put my entrepreneurial mind to work and began to put pencil to paper and drafted the initial Tally Bill ideas. These were simple ideas to solve this unconstitutional and systemic injustice within the VA. I also manufactured and laid out a blueprint as to how the tort claims process and system should work in a fair, just, and equitable manner for all veterans.

When all of this started to come together, the media caught wind of my story and picked it up and ran with it. This sparked a national news story that would soon help drive the bill, the mission, and the cause.

Several large media outlets reported on the story, and shortly thereafter it was picked up by 200 other TV stations across the country. The

story was also written and appeared online by at least a dozen media publication companies.

As my bill draft and plan began to come together, I recruited my own online legislative team to help me put everything into legal bill form, so that I could begin presenting this proposed Tally Bill to any and all members of Congress that were willing to listen. Within weeks my team and I were able to professionally draft, in legal congressional form, the very first version of the Tally Bill.

This was an extremely exciting moment as we now had a solution in hand, and we not only held the keys to addressing this seventy-four-year VA legal loophole but had the firepower we needed to fix it, all wrapped up in simple and easy to understand and read text that most if not all would call a common-sense solution.

Motivated and eager to get this immediately out to members of Congress, my legislative team got to work. Over the course of two weeks, we emailed nearly 200 sitting members of the 115th Congress, and unfortunately, we never heard back from one of them.

We were shut out, ignored, and passed over as if we were second-rate citizens in a country that simply did not care about the well-being of veterans and their honorable service to this nation.

And to add insult to injury, I did not even have a congressman to give me the voice in Washington that was needed to be heard to make a positive difference in the lives of the estimated 20.2 million American veterans.

I essentially became my own congressman, boarded a red-eye flight out of San Diego, and landed in Washington, DC, six hours later. Pain, anxiety, fear, and exhaustion riddled my broken body, but I knew I was on the path that God had chosen for me, albeit it was the path of the unknown.

I met my friend and fellow Marine brother John Steelman in DC later that day where he helped carry my bag, keep me company, strongly advocate on behalf of the Tally Bill, and ensure that I was not alone on this trip. John and I served together in the Marine Corps, and he insisted that he help with this mission. He promised

to add value to the cause and would essentially end up being a significant role player, and a driving force behind the success of the Tally Bill. John also gave me much needed counsel along the way, helped keep me grounded and focused, and always was there for me when I needed someone to talk to. Whether it was a frustrating day or creating content to share on our social media platforms, John was always there, and he brought a positive attitude. John is the embodiment of a United States Marine, and lives by the motto, *Semper Fi* through his actions.

Our first stop was meeting with the VA Office of General Counsel, as well as the United States deputy secretary of the VA. I was also now sitting across the table from the very man that denied my claim based on a technicality and in my opinion committed a fraudulent crime against my family and me. I was experiencing moments of grief and anger during our meeting, but never showed it or expressed it physically or verbally. I remained calm, cool, and collective.

This meeting was extremely nerve racking, as I had difficulty speaking because I was experiencing cognitive decline due to the heavy amounts of opioids and benzos my body had consumed over the years.

We were sure to keep the meeting 100 percent positive, professional, and friendly and to hand-deliver the solution in the form of a drafted bill to the office of the secretary of the VA. My plan was to get the VA to make an administrative law change to the Federal Tort Claims Act to close the loophole that destroyed me and the thousands of others before me.

By doing so, I was going to be as sincere and professional as possible to these high-ranking officials of the VA that agreed to meet with me. I

then explained to them in considerable detail that I was prepared to take this drafted proposed legislation to Capitol Hill to lobby for positive change. With my efforts I was hopeful to have a new law one day or we could just end the systemic problem right here, and right now, with an immediate administrative law change that would ensure the rights and protections of all veterans.

Even though I felt as if we had a great meeting, the VA officials respectfully declined my offer of making a change that would have closed the loophole and wished me "good luck on the Hill." John and I shook their hands and thanked them for the opportunity to sit down and discuss the details of the Tally Bill.

The very next morning, I woke up, loaded my pockets up with pain pills and anxiety medications, and hit the ground running. Upon my arrival to Capitol Hill, I was met by a news crew and did a quick media interview as to the importance of the bill, raise awareness and what my plan was.

The media would end up playing a monumental role throughout this process and brought this story the attention it deserved on a national stage.

I am not going to lie. It was a bit intimidating at first to take the main stage at the Capitol Rotunda for my first big TV interviews. I was surrounded by news cameras, members of Congress, and high-profile members of the press. I gathered myself, took a deep breath, and did as good of a job as I could. I prayed that I would get through the interviews without mumbling and deliver a sincere, positive, and consistent message to the viewers about this injustice I was working to correct within the Department of Veterans Affairs.

That morning I hand-delivered the first version of the Tally Bill to the steps of the Capitol building, entered the building, and walked the halls of Congress, going door to door urging lawmakers to change this outdated law that has destroyed the lives of veterans and their families for generations. I did this all to ensure that I would not be ignored any longer, and this was far too important to continually ignore and pretend to care.

I politely, professionally, and energetically engaged Congress

and simply asked them to listen—and to act! Some members listened, and others not so much. I was influential enough during my meetings as I lobbied my ideas and bill with great energy and empathy that I caught the attention of several members of Congress and one in particular, Representative Dave Brat. Rep. Dave Brat agreed with me and acknowledged there was a problem and agreed to introduce the Tally Bill.

His staff and I immediately hit it off, and we got to work. Within thirty days of my initial visit to Washington, DC, and meeting with some thirty congressional members and staffers, the Tally Bill was born and became an official bill with a bill number, H.R. 7105, and was formally introduced on the House floor by Congressman Dave Brat (R-VA) on October 30, 2018. The following is the official bill language on what the Tally Bill would do, and how it will change the way the Federal Tort Claims process works.

115TH CONGRESS
2D SESSION

H. R. 7105

To amend title 38, United States Code, to ensure that certain health care contractors of the Department of Veterans Affairs are subject to Federal tort claims laws, to improve the accountability of physicians of the Department, and for other purposes.

IN THE HOUSE OF REPRESENTATIVES

OCTOBER 30, 2018

Mr. Brat (for himself, Mrs. Comstock, Mrs. Radewagen, and Miss González-Colón of Puerto Rico) introduced the following bill: which was referred to the Committee on Veterans' Affairs

---

A BILL

To amend title 38, United States Code, to ensure that certain health care contractors of the Department of Veterans Affairs are subject to Federal tort claims laws, to improve the accountability of physicians of the Department, and for other purposes.

Be it enacted by the Senate and House of Representatives of the United States of America in Congress assembled,

SECTION 1. SHORT TITLE.

This Act may be cited as the "Brian Tally VA Medical Care and Liability Improvement Act".

SEC. 2. ACCOUNTABILITY OF HEALTH CARE PROVIDERS AT FACILITIES OF THE DEPARTMENT OF VETERANS AFFAIRS.

(a) Treatment Of Contractors Under Federal Tort Claims LAWS. —Section 7316 of title 38, United States Code, is amended by adding at the end the following new subsection:

"(g) (1) For purposes of this section, an individual who is not an employee of the Federal Government but who is authorized by the Secretary to provide health care or treatment at a facility of the Department pursuant to a contract or other agreement shall be treated as if the individual were a health care employee of the Administration with respect to the health care or treatment furnished by that individual in such a facility of the Department.

"(2) If an individual described in paragraph (1) is the defendant employee of a civil action or proceeding pursuant to this section, any claim of that individual for benefits under an insurance policy with respect to medical malpractice relating to such civil action or proceeding shall be subrogated to the United States.

"(3) (A) If an individual described in paragraph (1) is the defendant employee of at least three separate covered cases during a five-year period, the Secretary—

"(i) shall revoke the individual's authorization to provide health care or treatment at a facility of the Department; and

"(ii) may not enter into any contract or agreement that authorizes the individual to provide health care or treatment at a facility of the Department.

"(B) In this paragraph, the term 'covered case' means—

"(i) a civil action or proceeding pursuant to this section that resulted in a judgment against the United States; or

"(ii) such an action or proceeding that the United States compromises or settles, and the Secretary determines should be treated as a covered case for purposes of this paragraph.".

(b) NOTIFICATIONS AND OUTREACH REGARDING FEDERAL TORT CLAIMS. —Such section, as amended by subsection (a), is further amended by adding at the end the following new subsections:

"(h) Not later than 30 days following the date on which a judgment is entered against the United States in a civil action or proceeding pursuant to this section, the Secretary shall notify the following entities with respect to such judgment:

"(1) The appropriate licensing entity of each State in which a defendant employee is licensed as a health care professional.

"(2) The National Practitioner Data Bank established pursuant to the Health Care Quality Improvement Act of 1986 (42 U.S.C. 11101 et seq.).

"(i) The Secretary shall publish in a clear and conspicuous manner on the internet website of the Department an explanation of the rights of an individual under this section, including—

"(1) an explanation of the procedure to file an administrative claim pursuant to section 515 of this title or section 2675 of title 28.

"(2) the circumstances under which an individual may file a civil action or proceeding pursuant to this section; and

"(3) time limits that can bar recovery under this section.".

(c) ACCOUNTABILITY OF PHYSICIANS OF THE DEPARTMENT. —Section 7461 of such title is amended—

(1) in subsection (a), by adding at the end the following new sentence: "The Under Secretary shall bring such charges based on professional conduct or competence against a section 7401(1) employee who is the defendant employee of at least three separate

civil actions or proceedings pursuant to section 7316 of this title that, within a five-year period—

"(1) resulted in a judgment against the United States; or

"(2) (A) were compromised or settled by the United States; and

"(B) the Secretary determines should be counted under this sentence for purposes of bringing such charges."; and

(2) in subsection (c)(3), by adding at the end the following new subparagraph:

"(C) The provision of care subject to a civil action or proceeding pursuant to section 7316 of this title that—

"(i) resulted in a judgment against the United States; or

"(ii) is compromised or settled by the United States and the Secretary determines such care should be covered by this paragraph.".

(d) APPLICABILITY. —The amendments made by this section shall take effect with respect to actions or omissions covered under section 7316 of title 38, United States Code, occurring on or after the date of the enactment of this Act.

Now that we had a pulse and the credibility we needed, my team and I began to focus our efforts on veteran service organizations (VSOs), the House Committee on Veterans' Affairs, and all members of Congress who were actively serving on the VA Subcommittee on Health.

With an active congressional bill in hand, we were rallying support behind it as we called on members of Congress to put their weight and support behind H.R. 7105, also known as the Tally Bill, by signing on to the bill as cosponsors.

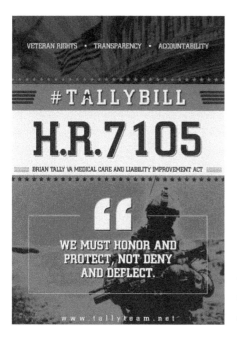

We knew the legislative calendar was dwindling by the day as we drew closer and closer to the 2018 election, and time was of the essence if the Tally Bill was to become law prior to the 115th Congress ending. We ramped up our marketing and awareness project with the help of hundreds of volunteers from across the country, and we made a ton of noise!

Eager to get this job done, we simultaneously began targeting all VSOs such as AMVETS (American Veterans), DAV (Disabled American Veterans), VFW (Veterans of Foreign Wars), TREA (The Enlisted Association), and dozens more to get them actively involved and fully engaged in our advocacy efforts. My first message was to the chief advocacy officer of AMVETS, a congressionally chartered national veteran service organization. I explained the loophole to him in depth and the significance of this crucial veteran legislation and asked them to help raise the awareness that was needed to bring this to the surface and expose the unlawful practices and procedures that were currently in place.

Immediately after hearing my story and my concerns, AMVETS publicly and formally put their weight behind the Tally Bill and became one of the closest and most influential allies we had.

> "We believe passage of this law will address the longstanding problem of breached due process for veterans who suffer disability, as well as survivors who lose loved ones, due to medical malpractice or negligence on the part of the Department of Veterans Affairs independent contractors."
>
> – AMVETS National Executive Director

SERVING WITH PRIDE

AMVETS

NATIONAL
HEADQUARTERS
4647 Forbes Boulevard
Lanham, Maryland
20706-4380
TELEPHONE: 301-459-9600
FAX: 301-459-7924
E-MAIL: amvets@amvets.org

November 28, 2018

The Honorable David Brat
1628 Longworth HOB
Washington, DC 20515

Re: Statement of Support for H.R. 7105, the Brian Tally VA Medical
Care and Liability Improvement Act

Dear Congressman Brat:

American Veterans (AMVETS), the most inclusive Congressionally
chartered veteran service organization in the U.S., supports the enactment
of H.R. 7105, the "Brian Tally VA Medical Care and Liability
Improvement Act." We believe passage of this law will address the
longstanding problem of breached due process for veterans who suffer
disability, as well as survivors who lose loved ones, due to medical
malpractice or negligence on the part of the Department of Veterans
Affairs independent contractors.

Suing the federal government, or one of its agencies, for a wrongful action
is an inherently complex and overwhelming process. But it becomes a
shell game when victims of medical malpractice are led to believe they
are dealing with a federal employee, only to find out later an independent
contractor committed the offense. When this happens, the independent
contractor's status as a non-agent of the government deceptively
immunizes the government from liability, leaving veterans or survivors
with no recourse.

Adding insult to veritable injury are the deceptive practices carried out on
the part of the government to subvert the harmed individual's due process
rights. Examples include stifling claims and withholding decisions until
the statute of limitations has expired and negotiating in bad faith when
discussing terms of settlement. This bill, if passed, will ensure greater
accountability and transparency in the delivery of healthcare to veterans
in cases where independent contractors are responsible for causing undue
harm to our Nation's veterans in the course of that care.

We thank you for sponsoring this important legislation and will implore
your colleagues in Congress to support the passage of H.R. 7105 as well,
for the sake of veterans who protected our country and now deserve our
best efforts to protect them.

Sincerely,

Joseph R. Chenelly
AMVETS National Executive Director

Within hours, I had a letter of support in my hand that was signed off by both the national executive director and the chief advocacy officer of AMVETS National. They penned the letter to Congress, and it immediately helped generate steam, credibility, and the awareness that was needed to help get this bill the attention it deserved.

Unfortunately, our legislative days were short-lived because the bill was introduced extremely late in the 115th Congress. My daughter Delaney thought she could help, so she got to work, all on her own doing. She understood that we had a bill recently introduced in congress and we were running out of time.

My little girl was probably the most affected by my story as she had a front-row seat to this horror show. She went to all of my appointments, watched as my wife took care of me, and she knew the daily struggles I had. She was my "ride or die," as she spent most of her time with me in my room, always in my presence and keeping me company. I would be in my chair, and she would be sitting on my walker or sitting on the bed right next to me.

We would watch TV together and talk about sports, art, and really anything that came up. She was my angel and always surrounded me in unconditional love.

One afternoon she came into the room, and she said, "Here you go, Dad. I wrote a letter to President Trump, and I want to go mail it."

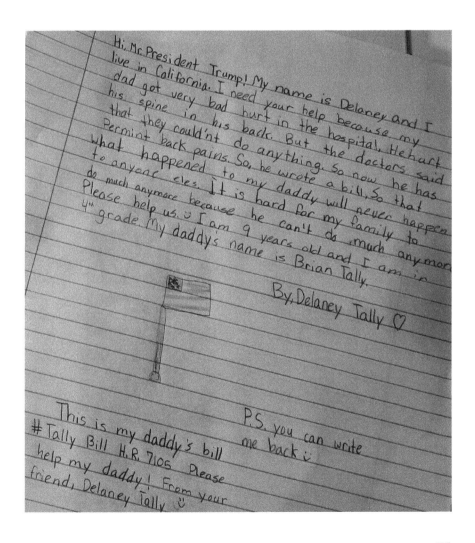

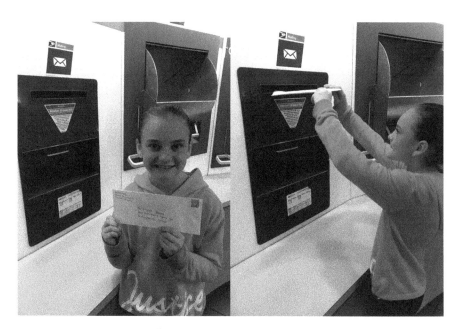

She was hopeful that he would receive it and pass the Tally Bill. She has always been a highly creative young lady, and she put together a very well thought out and beautiful collage, through the mind of a nine-year-old little girl.

She wanted her voice to be heard through her own message that she articulated and one that definitely spoke from her heart. It gave me so much joy and happiness and filled my heart with so much gratitude and love that she would do such a thing, and all on her own doing. We shared some tears, and I hugged her and did not let go, as this was the sweetest thing I had ever seen.

Unfortunately, President Trump or his staff never reached out after Delaney sent her letter to the White House, and unfortunately like most bills in Congress, our bill (H.R. 7105) would die in Congress, which meant we would have to start this process all over again in January 2019, after the 116th Congress was officially sworn in.

As the Tally Bill grassroots effort grew and grew, we began generating national and world-wide attention, primarily in the veteran and active-duty military communities. We began receiving Tally Bill support pictures from around the world to share on our social media page. We received literally dozens of them. It was a truly humbling experience and wonderful feeling, knowing that I had an army behind me, and I was not alone in this fight to protect our nation's veterans, and to make sure this historic veteran legislation successfully crossed the finish line!

The #TallyBill hashtag was being seen from all over the world, and the support we had grew tremendously every day!

From the USA to Iraq and Afghanistan. From Guatemala and Honduras to Paris, France. From the 2019 World Series to Super Bowl LIII! From Jamaica to Denmark, and many more! It was a great honor to receive so many awesome Tally Bill support pictures!

CHAPTER 14:

BACK TO SQUARE ONE, AND A SECOND TRIP TO DC

Here we were now in January 2019, essentially starting all over. My team and I gave it all we had and pushed extremely hard over the last six months, including sending hundreds of emails, countless phone calls, dozens of congressional office visits, and several VSO meetings. We had some solid building blocks in place, such as a letter of support, a successful trip to DC, and a formal bill introduction from the previous Congress. So, I was quite confident heading into this new Congress.

Every day I would start my morning with a cup of coffee and begin to fire off emails and phone calls and create social media content to further recruit volunteers and veteran advocates to help with this grassroots effort. I had transformed my once personal office into a full-blown congressional war room where I worked every day and carefully strategized my next moves as this was a game of chess I was playing, not checkers.

Before I knew it, the sun was going down, the day was over, and I had spent the entire day working on the bill. This was my life for well over two and a half years, all while battling my pain and maintaining all of my continual doctors' appointments. This was my obsession and was on my mind every second, every minute, every hour of every day, and nothing was going to get in my way!

Rest assured, I will never stop working hard on behalf of the estimated 20.2 million American veterans to ensure their rights and protections! "We are still grinding," and it is time to close the seventy-four-year VA

legal loophole that has destroyed the lives of veterans and their families for generations!

After my first trip to DC, a friend of mine suggested that I have a fundraiser to raise the funds that were needed to get back and forth from DC without further spending what little money we had left to fight on behalf of all veterans. That led to my team and me creating and launching a commemorative Tally Bill challenge coin.

They were made available online as we were accepting in-kind donations to help me out with airfare, hotel accommodations, food, and other items that were associated with this duty. The fundraiser would end up being a great success and helped keep me in front of Congress and would end up paying for two additional trips. Without the help and support of the hundreds and thousands of veterans, veterans' supporters, and every day average Americans, none of this would have ever been possible. I had dedicated my life to this mission, and I was going to see it all the way through!

In February 2019 I showed back up to the front steps of the Capitol building, greeting all the incoming freshman members of Congress and

reconnected with some previous members and staffers from last year's visit. I showed up with the same tenacious and positive efforts I delivered last time. It felt like *Groundhog Day*, and here I was once again filling my pockets up with pain pills and anxiety medications to get me through the day so I could continue to walk the halls of Congress, going door to door urging lawmakers to change this outdated law that has destroyed the lives of veterans and their families for generations.

Our meetings could not have been any better, and we were well received. When I enter a congressional meeting, I enter the room being fully prepared: a prewritten letter to the member(s) of Congress I am meeting with, an original copy of the Tally Bill draft, a copy of H.R. 7105, the AMVETS support letter, and a handwritten thank you card, all inside a professional folder.

We were extremely blessed and incredibly lucky to have had Ideal Print & Copy in Temecula reach out to me in an effort to help with my print and design needs when it came to marketing the Tally Bill.

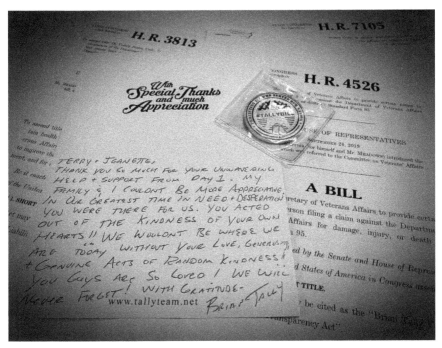

You see, I was a customer of theirs prior to my injury, and we had created a wonderful working relationship. Once they found out what happened to me and heard my story, they were locked in and became 100 percent engaged with whatever I needed and supplied this mission with high quality-colored flyers, folders, and thank you cards.

They were huge supporters of this cause and mission, and they fought and contributed right alongside me, and they would end up playing such a vital and monumental role throughout this process.

It was important to me to look and play the part of a professional lobbyist who could effectively lay out a solution in hard stock colored-print paper, along with folders and colored copies of the bills. Let's face it, I was essentially acting as my own member of congress, so I had to maintain the highest standards of professionalism and fit the part, or the role I was playing.

They made that a reality, and we were supplied with anything and everything we needed to effectively tell the story the way it deserved to be told, share the bills, and have it all displayed in a fashion that showed we were serious, and we were here to make things happen. Because of the professionalism we showed through the marketing material and flyers, the congressional staffers took us seriously, which led to bigger meetings with the actual reps themselves.

Before my injury and pitfall, I was a landscaper. As explained, I had no formal training in advocacy or lobbying Congress. I simply brought the same mindset and service I brought to my place of business every day and treated Congress as if they were my clients, in my place of business, essentially killing them with kindness and gratitude, so I could have the opportunity to tell not only my story but the story of thousands more and the challenges we have all faced as this generational loophole continued

to plague the Department of Veterans Affairs. I treated this as if it were my business; the only difference was it didn't come with a paycheck.

It was simply a calling, and it was being done all for the greater good of the country, so the suffering and the hardships that my family and I endured would never happen again. I began to turn my pain into a newfound purpose and found that reinventing one's self is definitely not an easy task, but in the end it will all have been worth the blood, sweat, tears, sacrifice, and pain! It was time to resurrect, rebuild, and reinvent!

As time went on, there was definitely a buzz that surrounded John and me as we walked the halls of Congress, meeting with anyone and everyone who would listen, even having impromptu meetings in the hallways, elevators, the congressional cafeteria, and even the lobby.

Very quickly we caught the attention of several members of Congress, one in particular, Mark Meadows of North Carolina. The former legislative staffer who worked for Congressman Dave Brat was now working as the legislative director for Congressman Mark Meadows, and he quickly became our greatest asset to this cause. He was instrumental in influencing Representative Meadows to not only support the Tally Bill but to be our congressional champion!

It did not take long or need much influence to show the systemic issues here and the timely importance of closing this criminal loophole as twenty million American veterans remained at risk. Without delay, Congressman Mark Meadows's legislative team and I drafted the second version of the Tally Bill, and it was formally introduced on July 17th, 2019. The bill number was H.R. 3813. The following is the official bill language, and what the law would do.

116TH CONGRESS
1ST SESSION

H. R. 3813

To amend title 38, United States Code, to ensure that certain health care contractors of the Department of Veterans Affairs are subject to Federal tort claims laws, to improve the accountability of physicians of the Department, and for other purposes.

IN THE HOUSE OF REPRESENTATIVES

JULY 17, 2019

Mr. Meadows (for himself and Mrs. Radewagen) introduced the following bill: which was referred to the Committee on Veterans' Affairs

---

A BILL

To amend title 38, United States Code, to ensure that certain health care contractors of the Department of Veterans Affairs are subject to Federal tort claims laws, to improve the accountability of physicians of the Department, and for other purposes.

Be it enacted by the Senate and House of Representatives of the United States of America in Congress assembled,

SECTION 1. SHORT TITLE.

This Act may be cited as the "Brian Tally VA Medical Care and Liability Improvement Act".

SEC. 2. ACCOUNTABILITY OF HEALTH CARE PROVIDERS AT FACILITIES OF THE DEPARTMENT OF VETERANS AFFAIRS.

(a) TREATMENT OF CONTRACTORS UNDER FEDERAL TORT CLAIMS LAWS. —Section 7316 of title 38, United States Code, is amended by adding at the end the following new subsection:

"(g) (1) (A) Except as provided by paragraph (2), this section shall not apply with respect to civil actions or other proceedings brought by an individual, or the estate of an individual, for damages for personal injury, including death, allegedly arising from malpractice or negligence of a non-Department provider if the Secretary notifies the individual, or the estate of the individual, of the following:

"(i) The involvement of the non-Department provider in the health care furnished to the individual.

"(ii) The nature of such health care furnished to the individual by the non-Department provider.

"(iii) The full name of the non-Department provider.

"(iv) The fact that the notification is made pursuant to this paragraph.

"(v) A statement that applicable State law may provide for a civil action or other proceeding by the individual, or the estate of the individual, against the non-Department provider, including information that specifies any statute of limitations for such applicable State law.

"(B) The Secretary shall make each notification under subparagraph (A) not later than 30 days after the date on which an individual or estate files a claim pursuant to section 2675 of title 28, United States Code. The Secretary shall make such notification using certified mail (with either return receipt requested or other means of verification that the notification was sent) to the individual or the estate, and to any attorney of the individual or the estate representing the individual or the estate with respect to such claim.

"(2) If the Secretary does not make the notification required by paragraph (1) during the period required by that paragraph with respect to civil actions or other proceedings brought by an individual, or the estate of an individual, for damages for personal injury, including death, allegedly arising from malpractice or negligence of a non-Department provider, the non-Department provider shall be treated as if the provider were a health care employee of the Administration with respect to the health care or treatment furnished by that provider in a facility of the Department to the individual.

"(3) If a non-Department provider described in paragraph (2) is the defendant employee of a civil action or proceeding pursuant to this section, any claim of that provider for benefits under an insurance policy with respect to medical malpractice relating to such civil action or proceeding shall be subrogated to the United States.

"(4) (A) If a non-Department provider described in paragraph (1) or (2) is the defendant employee of at least three separate covered cases during a five-year period, the Secretary—

"(i) shall revoke the provider's authorization to provide health care or treatment at a facility of the Department; and

"(ii) may not enter into any contract or agreement that authorizes the provider to provide health care or treatment at a facility of the Department.

"(B) The Secretary shall establish a process by which a non-Department provider may appeal an action under subparagraph (A).

"(5) In this subsection:

"(A) The term 'covered case' means any of the following:

"(i) A civil action or proceeding pursuant to this section that resulted in a judgment against the United States, or such an action or proceeding that the United States compromises or settles.

"(ii) A civil action or proceeding pursuant to State law for personal injury, including death, allegedly arising from malpractice or negligence that resulted in a judgment against a non-Department provider, or such an action or proceeding that the non-Department provider compromises or settles.

"(B) The term 'non-Department provider' means a health care provider who is not an employee of the Federal Government but who is authorized by the Secretary to provide health care or treatment at a facility of the Department pursuant to a contract or other agreement.".

(b) Notifications And Outreach Regarding Federal Tort Claims.—Such section, as amended by subsection (a), is further amended by adding at the end the following new subsections:

"(h) Not later than 30 days following the date on which a judgment is entered against the United States in a civil action or proceeding pursuant to this section, the Secretary shall notify the following entities with respect to such judgment:

"(1) The appropriate licensing entity of each State in which a defendant employee is licensed as a health care professional.

"(2) The National Practitioner Data Bank established pursuant to the Health Care Quality Improvement Act of 1986 (42 U.S.C. 11101 et seq.).

"(i) The Secretary shall publish in a clear and conspicuous manner on the internet website of the Department an explanation of the rights of an individual under this section, including—

"(1) an explanation of the procedure to file an administrative claim pursuant to section 515 of this title or section 2675 of title 28.

"(2) the circumstances under which an individual may file a civil action or proceeding pursuant to this section; and

"(3) time limits that can bar recovery under this section.".

(c) ACCOUNTABILITY OF PHYSICIANS OF THE DEPARTMENT.—Section 7461 of such title is amended—

(1) in subsection (a), by adding at the end the following new sentence: "The Under Secretary shall bring such charges based on professional conduct or competence against a section 7401(1) employee who is the defendant employee of at least three separate civil actions or proceedings pursuant to section 7316 of this title that, within a five-year period—

"(1) resulted in a judgment against the United States; or

"(2) were compromised or settled by the United States."; and

(2) in subsection (c)(3), by adding at the end the following new subparagraph:

"(C) The provision of care subject to a civil action or proceeding pursuant to section 7316 of this title that—

"(i) resulted in a judgment against the United States; or

"(ii) is compromised or settled by the United States.".

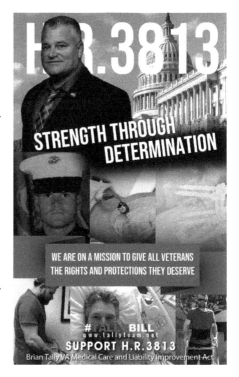

We now had action in the 116th Congress; however, Congressman Mark Meadows was a Republican who not only had strong ties to President Trump but was also considered to be a "firecracker" on the Hill as an outspoken conservative. That was good and bad for the Tally Bill. It was good because it gave the Tally Bill significant credibility that there was indeed a big problem that needed to be fixed, and his popularity on the

Republican side would definitely help drive this bill, mission and cause across the finish line.

On the other side, the bad news was he was not very popular or liked by many of the House Democrats, which would make it nearly impossible to have any co-sponsorship support from the Democrats, and thus far every cosponsor that signed on to this second version of the Tally Bill was a Republican.

So even though the bill language was very beautifully written, it was nonpartisan, and sought to close this seventy-four-year VA

legal loophole, the Democrats did not want to cross the aisle to sign on to Rep. Mark Meadows's legislation because it would give political points to not only the Meadows camp but also the GOP and President Trump, the man that all Washington DC Democrats hated.

So how was I supposed to get anything done in this political climate? It was easily the most divided Congress in US history, filled with egos, agendas, and pure hate. I carried on and promised myself to remain 100 percent impartial and nonpartisan on this important issue, as I did not want this to become political for all the wrong reasons.

My job was to positively and professionally engage with all members of Congress, despite their political preference, and have this pass the House on a bipartisan basis and become the voice of all veterans, who represent all walks of life that include Republican, Democrat, white, black, brown, male, female, gay, straight, and every socioeconomic background. The veteran community represents all of America and what America stands for. It's what makes us the greatest country in the world. This is when I kicked off yet another advocacy campaign, dubbed "You have a voice, and we need it"!

This call to action was also extraordinarily successful because we had all of the work done for folks. All letters were prewritten and could easily be found on our website. While there the constituent selected their member of Congress, filled in some basic information, and boom, it was sent via email. The estimated count of emails that were sent during this cause is likely to be in the 5,000-email range.

With that being said, I owed it to every veteran in the country to represent them all with fairness and kindness and in a nonpartisan fashion. I had to get to work, and I had to move quickly if we were going to have law in the 116th Congress.

Brian Tally after an exhausting week on Capitol Hill

CHAPTER 15:
THE HUNT FOR A DEMOCRAT COSPONSOR

Every second, every minute, every hour of every day, this mission was on my mind, and it became an obsession. I transformed my once landscape business office at my home into a legislative war room, and this is where I spent nearly 11,000 logged hours making phone calls, sending emails, creating social media content, recruiting advocates and volunteers, and strategizing my next move.

Essentially, I was my very own in-house congressman, except this nonpaying job did not come with any rewards or benefits. This work and mission were surely not for the faint of heart. I would work for days on end at a time, then my body would shut down. My eyes would be swollen shut, and my pain levels would intensify to the point where I spent the next several days in bed.

This was the life, and cycle that I lived for many years, and believe me, the debilitating pain plagued my body, mind, and spirit. I always did my best to keep a smile on my face for my little ones, especially as their leader, even when smiling was difficult to do.

The amount of anxiety, anger, emotional roller coasters, dead ends, and flat-out being ignored by so many people led to some brutally dark days of helplessness and hopelessness. What many did not see is the life of physical pain and struggle I lived with, and still do on an everyday basis.

The pain at times was unbearable, which is why I got routine spinal treatments and injections, which continues to this day. This was all

going on simultaneously with me pushing the Tally Bill. When I look back on it now, I have no idea how I endured it. All I can say is that it was God fighting alongside me in this battle and guiding me every step of the way. There is no other way to explain it. It was truly remarkable. I always knew and understood the definitions of words like *perseverance* and *resilience*. But I never knew what it meant to live it and go through it as I had never faced adversity and the challenges I was now facing. Well, I can say that I do now and have proven so through my direct actions of pure strength through determination, and never giving up, against all odds!

After these procedures I was doing everything I could do to just put one foot in front of the other. There were tough days, but I always hoped for a good positive outcome in the future. Until then I continued fighting and pushed through the pain and took it all, one day at a time!

Even though I had shown some great success thus far, it was still filled with so much anxiety and the fear of failing. That was my downfall,

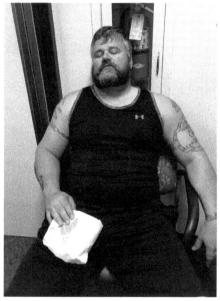

and it was also my driving force behind this bill. Yes, I struggled mightily, but we all struggle. It is how you handle your struggles that will define who you are and the legacy you will ultimately leave behind! I chose to be an example for my children, as I knew they were watching me.

My actions today will be their actions and decisions of tomorrow. If they watch their father quit, then I would be setting a bad example. I had to show that, no matter what, you must hang in there and take it all in stride and just get 1 percent better each and every day. This was all easier said than done obviously, but it is something that I used to motivate me. Nothing motivates me more than my family!

There were several times where I worked this mission so hard and I put so much pressure on myself that it made me sick, and I would have panic attacks that led to hospitalizations.

I was pushing my body to the point of complete exhaustion and collapse. My mind wanted to be the old Brian, but my body was faced with the crippling reality that my body had now been destroyed on the inside, and I would have to learn with dealing with physical and emotional pain for the rest of my life.

After a series of hospitalizations and a never-say-die attitude, I went right back to work to finish what I started, doing this all in a state of pain. Although at times I looked fine on the outside, on the inside I was a broken man, spiritually, mentally, and physically.

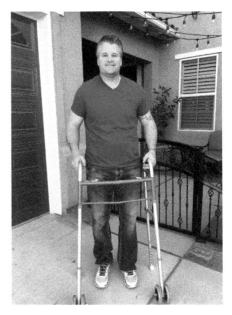

As I put my issues aside, I began to dwindle down my search for a Democrat sponsor in my immediate living area in Southern California. Some would say I was a glutton for punishment, but I just called it unfinished business. I was going to get this job done even if it killed me. That is how much I believed in this cause.

I began to drive and travel out to several outlying congressional districts in Southern California, and I would perform spot visits the same way I did in DC. I was dressed for the occasion and showed up ready to represent my bill the way it deserved to be, all in a suit and tie, prepared statements, a copy of my story, a thank you letter, and a copy of the Tally Bill all nicely placed into a professionally made legislation folder.

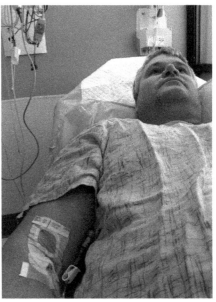

I knew if this nearly impossible task were going to get done, I would need to stand out, stand up, and have my voice heard.

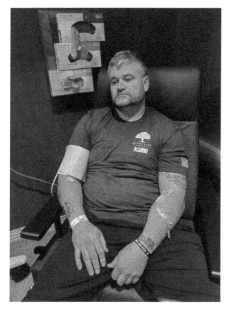

Over the next several months, I made significant strides and progress, meeting with several members of Congress and attending both in-person and telephone town halls. One of the most memorable town hall meetings I attended was Congressman Mark Takano's. Not only was he the congressman in Riverside, California, a neighboring city next to me, but he was also a vital part of this extremely complicated congressional puzzle.

He was also the acting chairman of the House Committee on Veterans' Affairs and was essentially the man we needed to have in our corner if we were going to advance the Tally Bill forward. He was also a Democrat, which would help us tremendously as the House was a Democrat majority.

I pushed as hard as I could on Congressman Mark Takano and leaned on his staff as much as I possibly could. I also attended local townhall meetings and literally reached out to his staff every day, asking for his support and for a House VA Committee hearing so I could testify and have my statement read and seen in the *Congressional Record* and ensure that my voice would be heard. I knew if I could get that opportunity, there was absolutely no way that they could say no. The story and the loophole were that egregious.

I also began to focus my efforts on a freshman member of Congress, Representative Mike Levin, from California's 49th congressional district, which was a neighboring district of mine in Southern California. I explained to him and his staff that I did not have a voice in Washington DC, and I desperately needed one as I did not have a congressman of my own. Boy, what are the odds, right?

I began to attend his telephone and social media town halls plus LIVE and in-person town halls. I acted and became heavily involved in making it a habit to make

contact with his staff daily and to start laying the foundation and putting together the pieces that were necessary to create a lasting and unforgettable relationship.

Again, I lived in the only district in the United States of America without a sitting member of Congress, and we still had action in the nation's capital on doing the very job that Congress had neglected to do for seven decades. I also explained in detail that I had two bills recently introduced in Congress and that I needed a local champion to get

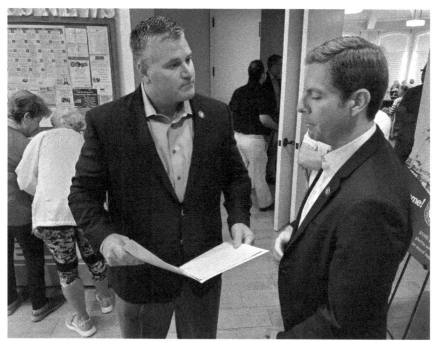

involved in the Tally Bill, give the voiceless a voice, and essentially cross the aisle and do whatever it took to get this bill passed.

Through months of calls, negotiations, and compromise, I finally had my third bill drafted, and it was ready to be introduced. The good news was Congressman Mike Levin was a Democrat, and we needed a Democrat very badly to pass the House; however, he did not want to sign on to Congressman Mark Meadows's version of the Tally Bill because he thought having his own version would have a better shot of passing the Democrat-controlled house.

He was also a sitting member on the House VA Committee, so Rep. Mike Levin's weight behind his own bill could be extremely beneficial to the ultimate successful passage of the Tally Bill. However, Mike Levin's team and I both knew that we did not want to introduce this third version of the Tally Bill without a Republican sponsor on it, or else it would be neglected and ignored like my other two bills were because they were Republican led.

So, I got to work and called our number one congressional ally in the house, Congressman Mark Meadows. I had built a great relationship with the legislative director over the course of the 115th and 116th Congress, and I pleaded with his legislative director to please sign on to this third bill that Rep. Mike Levin was getting ready to formally introduce, and we did not stand a chance without a strong Republican. After weeks of negotiations, and draft legislative language modifications, and amendments, the legislative director and Representative Meadows both agreed to cross the aisle. On September 26th, 2019, together they co-introduced and championed the "Brian Tally VA Employment Transparency Act." This will also be known as H.R. 4526. Here is the bill language and what the law would do.

116TH CONGRESS
1ST SESSION

H. R. 4526

To direct the Secretary of Veterans Affairs to provide certain notice to a person filing a claim against the Department of Veterans Affairs for damage, injury, or death on Standard Form 95.

IN THE HOUSE OF REPRESENTATIVES

SEPTEMBER 26, 2019

Mr. Levin of California (for himself and Mr. Meadows) introduced the following bill: which was referred to the Committee on Veterans' Affairs

A BILL

To direct the Secretary of Veterans Affairs to provide certain notice to a person filing a claim against the Department of Veterans Affairs for damage, injury, or death on Standard Form 95.

Be it enacted by the Senate and House of Representatives of the United States of America in Congress assembled,

SECTION 1. SHORT TITLE.

This Act may be cited as the "Brian Tally VA Employment Transparency Act".

SEC. 2. DEPARTMENT OF VETERANS AFFAIRS REQUIREMENT TO PROVIDE CERTAIN NOTICE TO PERSONS FILING CLAIMS FOR DAMAGE, INJURY, OR DEATH ON STANDARD FORM 95.

Not later than 30 days after the date on which a person submits to the Secretary of Veterans Affairs a claim for damage, injury, or death on Standard Form 95, or any successor form, the Secretary shall provide to the claimant notice of each of the following:

(1) The importance of securing legal counsel, including a recommendation that the claimant should secure legal counsel.

(2) The employment status of any individual listed on the form.

(3) If the claim involves a contractor that entered into an agreement with the Secretary, the statute of limitations regarding the claim in the State in which the claim arose.

This was a monumental breakthrough, and we now had significant momentum that began to snowball into a grassroots effort to "Rally around Tally" and accomplish the very mission we set sail on some two years ago. As the days, weeks, and months passed, we got closer and closer to our end goal. Now that we had our third bill formally introduced in Congress, it was time to fight, advocate, and lobby for my congressional hearing in the House Committee on Veterans' Affairs, because if it would not pass out of the committee, we would never have law. I remained laser focused and steadfast in my resolve.

I began to hold several "Call to Action" events each week. I welcomed everyone to participate and asked them to donate five minutes of their time each week to advocate on behalf of the Tally Bill. The "Call to Action" fliers were laid out very well, detailed with a script, the objective, the list of US Representatives we were targeting for that specific week, along with the direct phone numbers to the Washington DC offices. The goal was to make this as painless, and seamless as possible for our volunteers to easily contribute to this cause and get involved without taking too much of their time, as I understood people are busy. This was the most effective way that I could get the masses involved and get the phones ringing inside the offices of these targeted representatives.

These "Call to Actions" were so effective we conducted them every week for nearly six months. The objective stayed the same, and all we had to do is change the names and numbers of the next target group of representatives for that week. At the end of the week, I would sincerely thank everyone for their efforts, and for participating in the "Call to

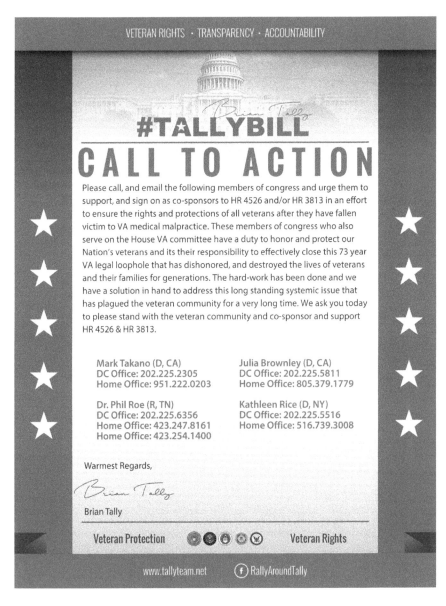

Action" events and energetically applauded them for doing their part in making a positive difference in the lives of all veterans.

In my eyes, this is what America is all about, and it was civic duty at its finest! In my opinion there was nothing more patriotic and fulfilling

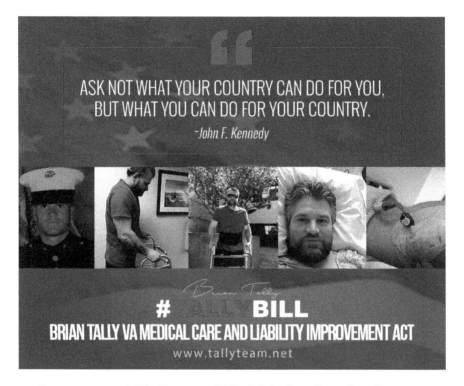

ASK NOT WHAT YOUR COUNTRY CAN DO FOR YOU,
BUT WHAT YOU CAN DO FOR YOUR COUNTRY.
~John F. Kennedy

TALLY BILL
BRIAN TALLY VA MEDICAL CARE AND LIABILITY IMPROVEMENT ACT
www.tallyteam.net

*Representatives Mike Levin and Mark Meadows Introduce Bipartisan
Legislation to Support Veterans with Legal Claims Against VA*

than citizen advocacy and getting people involved in a positive manner. It was also a creative way to connect with people from all over the country and it gave everyone their own opportunity to be a part of this journey and play their very own role in this process. If we were going to achieve this goal, I knew it would take a village and it would take the masses, working in conjunction to get this job done. It was certainly something I could not do solely on my own, as this would need to be a TEAM effort.

Many folks have asked me over the years, how do I keep going or even have the energy to deal with the largest and most powerful bureaucracy in the United States of America? I say it is simple. There is a great need for positive change, and the only way to create necessary positive change is to put yourself right in the middle of it and get involved! A famous quote from former President John F. Kennedy says this, "Ask not what your country can do for you—ask what you can do for your country."

This quote helped me in more ways than one, and further reminded me that we have a duty and an obligation as citizens of the United States of America to stand up and let your voices be heard.

> **Washington, D.C.** – U.S. Representative Mike Levin (D-CA), member of the House Veterans' Affairs Committee, and Mark Meadows (R-NC) introduced the bipartisan *Brian Tally VA Employment Transparency Act* to support veterans with legal claims against the Department of Veterans Affairs or its contractors. The bill is named after Marine Veteran Brian Tally, who was denied the opportunity to file a medical malpractice claim due to a lack of transparency and efficiency at the VA. The VA failed to inform Tally that his doctor was a contractor and that his claim had to be filed in state court until after the statute of limitations had expired.
>
> The *Brian Tally VA Transparency Act* requires the VA, within 30 days of a veteran submitting a claim, to provide notice of the importance of securing legal counsel; the employment status of any individual involved in the claim; and the statute of limitations in the relevant state if the claim involves a contractor.
>
> "Veterans who have sacrificed for our country deserve the highest quality health care, and they should have every opportunity to seek recourse if they are harmed as a result of substandard medical treatment," said **Representative Levin**. "No veteran should have to experience what Brian Tally went through. This bill will help ensure that veterans receive the information they need to make timely decisions about their legal options, and I am grateful to Congressman Meadows for his partnership on this effort."

"We owe our veterans the absolute best healthcare we can provide, so it's both heartbreaking and unacceptable to read about stories like that of Brian Tally," said **Representative Meadows.** "What happened to Brian, and others like him, must never be allowed to happen again. It is our responsibility to make sure we provide our veterans all of the information they need to make quick, informed decisions about their healthcare, and hold our government accountable to make sure we get our servicemembers high quality care. I want to thank my colleague,

Rep. Levin, for his partnership on this effort—as well as Brian Tally for his leadership on bringing attention to such a critical need. My hope is that with this bill, we can take another step in that process of better stepping up to serve our veterans."

"I am deeply grateful for this bipartisan effort to increase accountability and transparency within the VA," said **Marine Veteran Brian Tally.** "Veterans who receive treatment at VA hospitals and clinics must have the information they need to file medical malpractice or negligence claims when necessary. This bill is a huge step toward closing a loophole that has prevented veterans and their families from receiving justice, and I am hopeful that more Democrats and Republicans will come together for the "Good of the Country" like Congressmen Levin and Meadows have done in an effort to pass this extremely important veteran legislation."

In January 2016, Brian Tally began experiencing debilitating back pain, and sought care at the Loma Linda VA. The doctor diagnosed him with a lower back sprain, denied a blood test or MRI, and prescribed painkillers. In March 2016, his family paid for an MRI outside of VA, which revealed he had been given a near-fatal misdiagnosis. Instead of a lower back sprain, Tally had structural damage to his back, and his ensuing surgery revealed a bone-eating staph infection that was destroying his spine.

Tally filed a tort claim with VA for medical malpractice and gross neglect. After nearly a year, he was told that the doctor was not a VA employee, but an independent contractor, so he would need to file in state court. At that point, the statute of limitations had passed, leaving Tally and his family without any options for recourse over the suffering he experienced. The bipartisan Brian Tally VA Employment Transparency Act would help prevent that from happening to any other veterans.

Rep. Levin, Mike [D-CA-49]

H.R. 4526
BRIAN TALLY VA EMPLOYMENT TRANSPARENCY ACT

Veterans who have sacrificed for our country deserve the highest quality health care, and they should have every opportunity to seek recourse if they are harmed as a result of substandard medical treatment

~*Congressman Mike Levin*

VETERANS RIGHTS · TRANSPARENCY · ACCOUNTABILITY

#TALLYBILL

www.tallyteam.net

CHAPTER 16:

THE TALLY BILL ROAD SHOW 2020

AFTER YEARS OF BATTLE, ADVO-cacy, letters, calls, emails, town halls, and constituent support from across the country, the House Committee on Veterans' Affairs agreed to hear my bill, and I was granted a formal invite to attend an open session and participate in the legislative hearing on H.R. 4526, also known as the *Brian Tally VA Employment Transparency Act*, on March 25, 2020. I was so excited and relieved to have finally been given this moment to tell my story and speak in front of Congress, personally urging lawmakers to close

this seventy-four-year VA legal loophole that has destroyed and dishonored the lives of veterans and their families for generations.

You see, this job did not come with a paycheck, and when you work so hard day in and day out, typically at the end of the week you will be rewarded with a paycheck. There was no paycheck or reward at the end of the week for me, just unreturned phone calls, and emails. I had

no boss encouraging me, or guiding me, or showing me. I had to teach myself everything I knew thus far about this new world I found myself in and it was very frustrating at times. My entrepreneurial mind spirit helped keep me grounded, discipline and moving forward in a positive direction every day. My rewards all came in the form of bill introductions, and hearings. It was always a great day when we had a new cosponsor sign on to the bills, or even new media stories

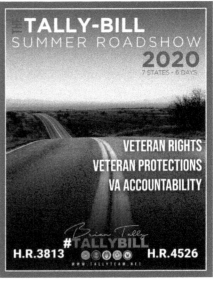

that came out to help drive awareness. Those were my rewards to keep me engaged, self-motivated, and on mission. It was not easy, and it took

a lot of discipline. Every day was filled with life lessons and new experiences.

This was not a job, it was a calling of mine, and I did everything in my power to honorably and courageously answer that call to service and fight for the good of the country. This had become a life goal of mine to change this outdated and unconstitutional law.

I did not waste any time in securing my airfare and hotel accommodations. I immediately began to plan and build my itinerary around the hearing. While I was there, the plan was to meet with some additional members of Congress and their staff to get as many cosponsors as we could get to sign on to the Tally Bill. Then guess what? You got it…yet another roadblock and brick wall in my way! Now we had a pandemic on our hands!

Unfortunately, due to the COVID-19 outbreak, the Capitol building would be closed to visitors, and my trip was canceled.

As my luck would have it, I finally wanted to get up and out of my old raggedy chair, where I lived for years, and begin to live life again. I really did not have a choice because it broke and ended up falling apart anyway due to the overuse of it anyways. Heck, I lived there for about three years straight. That's right, three years of my life, wasting away in a damn chair.

With that being said, I could not let the forward momentum we had get lost and forgotten as a pandemic blanketed our country and the world, so I launched an awareness project dubbed the 'Tally Bill Summer Roadshow 2020,' I packed a bag, and I hit the road. COVID-19 was not going to stop me or this mission!

I did not let the COVID-19 pandemic slow me down. I put together a plan and strategically mapped out a seven-state Tally Bill tour to get out and raise awareness about the bills and to drum up as much support as possible.

So, I hit the road, visiting every congressional district in my path. I made dozens of unannounced visits to congressional offices, dropped off Tally Bill flyers and folders, and stopped in every local veteran's hall along the way. My mission was to raise awareness on veterans' rights and protections and closing a seventy-four-year VA legal loophole.

The road trip helped me so much mentally and emotionally. It was the first time in nearly four years that I had gotten out and was feeling a sense of happiness again, some self-worth, pride, and from this point on, I slowly started building up my confidence again. I had the chance to meet new friends and reconnect and spend some time with some of my lifelong friends. It was all good for the soul.

This was all happening simultaneously as most people throughout the world all went indoors and shut themselves out. I continued on with the plan anyways, and it ended up being a phenomenal experience and a memorable trip well worth taking.

I successfully generated more congressional support from across the country, and I delivered awareness to hundreds of veterans through the

course of some impromptu events where I spoke. On a moment's notice, I had the Colorado Springs TREA veteran's hall set up and ready to go for an evening event where we had about 50 people attend. I was fortunate enough to speak at three VFW halls along the journey as well.

I even had the opportunity to be interviewed live on-air in several states during my trip to further discuss the Tally Bill legislation, what I was doing to raise awareness, how my Tally Bill road trip was going, and ultimately how I was educating all veterans on the loophole and how it worked, so all veterans would have some mental awareness of the loophole in case one of them found themselves or a loved one trapped in it prior to having the Tally Bill signed into law!

CHAPTER 17:
MY CONGRESSIONAL HEARING

THROUGHOUT THIS ENTIRE PAINSTAKING PROCESS, ONE THING REMAINED the same, and I never wavered from the plan! Not even a little bit! The plan from day one was to design and build my own blueprint through my daily experiences. I constructed it as I went through everyday motions and gained further knowledge, whether it was on Capitol Hill, on the phone, or sending emails. It seemed to be working, so I trusted the process and continued to advance forward.

Though it was repetitive, it was necessary, and I had to do what I had to do to effectively drill it in the heads of Congress in a way that made sense, was short, and was easily understood.

There was not a blueprint available for me to follow, as this type of veteran/citizen advocacy had never been done before with the circumstances of my story, so again, I built my own.

The most important thing I learned was to stay on topic, and on point without veering off subject or the task at hand. The mission remained the same and that was changing a seventy-four-year VA legal loophole that has destroyed the lives of veterans and their families for generations!

The Solution I brought to the table was the "Tally Bill,". This law would ensure the rights and protections of all veterans! Positive Energy = Positive Results, and that's what was keeping me successful and in front of the decision makers that could make this law change.

Finally, after four months we had the congressional hearing we all had been anxiously and patiently waiting for. The pandemic had put

everything behind schedule, and Congress was being pulled in every direction possible. But we had it, and it was a success.

Yes, it was another major setback and barrier that stood in our way, but we accepted that and continued on with the mission in other creative ways such as the road trip I took.

When the pandemic hit, I had another "out" and option to just say, "I'm done," and simply walk away. Though quitting seemed very appealing, it was never really an option for me. I could not live with myself knowing that I surrendered all of my hard work and tenacious efforts and walked away during the most intense battle of my life and let this egregious loophole continue to live on and destroy more and more families. I could not abandon the mission and the most important and purposeful fight of my life.

I submitted my statement that was read into the *Congressional Record* on July 23, 2020. Now more than ever we needed the Tally Bill legislation to be passed to protect all veterans!

During normal times we have a great deal of medical malpractice and gross negligence that occurs within the VA. Now, with an influx of patients at all VA hospitals and clinics due to the COVID-19 pandemic, there will be an overwhelming amount of neglect and malpractice that will occur; and I was going to use this to my advantage.

Malpractice and negligence will be on the rise, especially now because our health care system has been overwhelmed and is currently bogged down! Mistakes can and will happen! It is inevitable.

And as I have always said, when tragedy strikes in the form of VA medical malpractice, there must be transparency, accountability, and protective measures put in place. This will and should always include the employment status of the clinicians that are treating you when they have been named in a federal tort claim, and this rightful information should always be furnished in a timely manner.

The hearing went very well, especially when Rep. Mike Levin put the VA on blast, asking some incredibly good questions that the VA could not give an explanation or answer to, and they later stated they were having technical difficulties and left the meeting.

This tactic lacked transparency, backbone, and professionalism, just as my family and I had been treated thus far by the VA's Office of General Counsel. It just goes to show you if they treat members of Congress this way, just imagine how they are treating an at-risk population with vulnerable veterans that are going through some of their toughest and most challenging times. The chairman of the House Committee on Veterans' Affairs, agreed with me and further went on to say that the "VA must be transparent to the veterans they serve."

Without further delay the Tally Bill was passed in the House and was headed to the United States Senate.

Immediately following the hearing, we had a breakthrough moment, and I released an endless flow of tears as I proudly watched and listened to this congressional hearing LIVE on my computer.

My heart was racing, I was visibly shaking, and I began recounting the last four and a half years up to the moment of time I was currently living in! The hard work that my team and I put into this cause and mission was beginning to take shape.

After the hearing I did not know what to say, other than thanking God for answering my prayers and giving me the energy and the passion to never quit and always keep pushing forward, no matter how hard the climb may be or the obstacles that stood in my way! Thank you for opening up doors and putting the right people in my life.

I also thanked my wife and kids with endless gratitude for allowing me to be consumed by thousands of hours of endless congressional work, day in and day out! They knew what this meant to me, and they were there with me and encouraging me every step of the way.

This was an extremely emotional moment for me, and I had to step away for the next week or so to collect myself and my excitement, gather my thoughts, and calm down my jitters.

I knew we were not done yet; however, this was another step in the right direction and an award, if you will, to keep me laser focused and hungry for more. This was an example of thousands of tiny steps equaling one large step, and again, I gained the confidence I needed to just hang in there and trust the process, even though at times I had lost all faith in our system.

We couldn't have accomplished this major milestone without the Tally Bill team, supporters, fellow veterans, and everyday American citizens being a part of such a positive grassroots effort and cause that will ensure the rights and protections of all veterans!

> Here is a statement put out by Rep. Mike Levin after the bill passed in the US House of Representatives.
> "Veterans who have sacrificed for our country deserve the highest quality health care, and they should have every opportunity to seek recourse if they are harmed as a result of substandard medical treatment," said Levin.
> "The VA Employment Transparency Act ensures that veterans have the information they need to make timely decisions about their legal options, so they never experience what Brian Tally went through. I am proud that this important bill passed unanimously through the House Veterans' Affairs Committee."
> "Despite the continual objections from VA leadership, this has not turned into a major roadblock for Tally on Capitol Hill. His sheer will, and tenacity alone will get this bill passed!"

Here is my official statement that was put into the *Congressional Record* and was read in front of the House Committee on Veterans' Affairs.

UNITED STATES HOUSE OF REPRESENTATIVES
VETERANS AFFAIRS COMMITTEE
JULY 23, 2020
STATEMENT FOR THE RECORD

WRITTEN AND PREPARED BY:
BRIAN J. TALLY, UNITED STATES MARINE CORPS
VETERAN ADVOCATE

Chairman Takano, Ranking Member Roe, and distinguished members of the House Veterans Affairs Committee; I come before you today to urge you to please close a 74-year VA Legal Loophole that has destroyed the lives of Veterans and their families for generations. I sincerely want to thank you for this opportunity and invitation to submit a statement for the record today, and to share my position regarding H.R. 4526, also referred to as the "Tally Bill." This is an extremely important piece of Veteran Legislation that is imperative to the wellbeing of every Veteran in this country. Nobody is immune to medical malpractice and negligence. We are all humans, and humans make mistakes. However, when tragedy strikes in the form of VA medical malpractice there must be accountability, transparency, and safeguards effectively put in place to protect those Veterans injured as a result of these mistakes. H.R. 4526 will do just that. It will provide the injured Veteran with rightful information in a timely manner to include the employment status of the accused clinician(s) so the injured Veteran can make informed and timely decisions after suffering personal injury by either VA negligence or wrongful actions within VA hospitals and clinics. Veterans deserve a fair and equitable system similar to the private sector, instead of a system full of legal loopholes that is stacked against them in every way possible.

SUMMARY

WHAT IS THE FEDERAL TORT CLAIMS ACT? Since its enactment in 1946, the Federal Torts Claims Act (FTCA) has been the legal mechanism for compensating people who have suffered personal injury by the negligent or wrongful action of employees of the US government. The FTCA permits an individual to bring a lawsuit directly against the federal government for certain VA-caused injury or death, when that individual has suffered damages, personal injury, or death due to the negligent actions of a federal government employee or agency acting within the scope of employment.

Federal law determines who is an "employee" vs. "independent contractor" but the scope of employment issues under the FTCA are decided by the state law of occurrence. The FTCA defines "employee of the government" to include "officers or employees of any federal agency…and persons acting on behalf of a federal agency in an official capacity, temporarily or permanently in the service of the United States." Many VA hospitals and facilities currently hire independent contractors to perform medical procedures and provide health care. These individuals are not considered government employees therefore any malpractice claims will not give rise to a claim under the FTCA. The government often denies liability and contends that the alleged negligence was not caused by an employee but an independent contractor. This legal defense is highly effective unless dealt with adequately, as VA medical centers frequently contract with private universities or hospitals for physicians. In each situation, the Office of General Counsel must isolate the portion of work out of which the claim arose. If an employer-employee relationship is present, the government is held liable. If the injury was caused by an independent contractor, the government is not liable. The independent contractor can still be sued in their private capacities in state court but not under the FTCA.

The FTCA's definition of "government employee" includes officers and employees of federal agencies, but specifically excludes "any contractor with the United States." 28 U.S.C. § 2671. Thus, the independent contractor exception to the FTCA often bars federal government liability and denies FTCA protection to the defendant party. The independent contractor is thereby liable for damages as a private citizen.

I will now lay out my story and statement of facts on how this law is ruining the lives of Veterans because it has turned into a "legal loophole" and is no longer working in the way it was intended to work since its creation in 1946. A lot has changed over the last 74 years pertaining to independent contractors working within VA hospitals and clinics across the country. Therefore, immediate legislative correction is needed without further delay to ensure the rights and protections of all Veterans.

THE VA LEGAL LOOPHOLE THAT RUINED MY LIFE AND SET ME ON A MISSION

Many thoughts ran through my mind during a fateful visit to a Department of Veterans Affairs (VA) emergency room. One of them was not, "Is this doctor who's treating me an independent contractor or government employee?" But this would turn out to be perhaps the most critical question, secondary only to what was causing the excruciating pain that brought me to my knees in my most desperate time of need.

In January 2016, my life changed in ways that I could have never seen coming or ever imagined. I endured grueling pain, bed soaking night sweats, and endless hours of lying on the cold bathroom floor desperately seeking any sort of relief. After multiple trips to the emergency room and an x-ray, I was injected with Dilaudid, Toradol, and Kenalog and was given a diagnosis of a "low back sprain" and sent home with a cocktail of pain pills.

This would continue for (4) months until surgery was finally approved because my wife paid out of pocket for an MRI to prove to the VA that something was medically wrong inside my spine. To the surgeon's surprise, as I lay open on the operating table, he found the cause of my pain—a bone-eating staph infection that was aggressively attacking my spine and was destroying my spinal bone, tissue, discs, nerves, and internal organs. An infection that would have been detected much earlier had the emergency room clinician(s) ordered a simple blood test and an MRI. In the (4) months I waited for my surgery in excruciating pain no blood tests or diagnostic testing was performed. I am incredibly lucky to have survived such an ordeal.

Once we realized that this untreated and near-fatal infection led to a host of other residual medical diagnoses, and I would be left with permanent injuries, my family and I decided to file a claim under the Federal Tort Claims Act (FTCA) for medical malpractice and gross negligence. Six months into the claims process, I began to receive calls from the VA's

General Counsel's office. The VA attorneys would repeatedly admit that the "VA failed to meet the standard of care and there was a breach in liability" and they were working on settling our claim. We were asked to be patient as "this is a very long and tiring process." They appeared very sincere, apologetic, and to show a great deal of compassion.

These optimistic calls of certainty came at our most desperate, and vulnerable times of need and they continued on for several months as we tried everything, we could to stave off complete financial ruin. They already had me physically beat up, battered, and hanging on for dear life due to the life changing medical malpractice injuries that will put most if not all victims in a state of incapacitation.

Then depression, anxiety, and hopelessness set in as my family and I completely shifted into survival mode and tried to comprehend and fully understand just how things went south so fast, while remaining hopeful that compensation would soon be coming to recoup a lifetime of lost earning potential.

Meanwhile the mortgage is late, credit card debt is stacking up, kids need clothes, food on the table, car payments, the bills are all still due, and now the injured veteran is no longer working due to the severe injuries sustained by the incompetency of several clinician(s).

Then the bombshell dropped. Nearly one year into the claims process, we received a letter stating that the VA was not responsible for the medical malpractice and gross negligence. The reason given: The clinician who made the error(s) was not a VA employee, rather an independent contractor working within the VA, and behind the VA veil, thus the Federal Tort Claims Act did not apply.

This meant my only recourse was to sue the clinician in state court for damages. However, by the time the VA "conveniently" revealed this crucial information the California state statute of limitations had expired by mere days. It seemed as if the Office of General Counsel had already strategized this outcome and were able to cherry-pick the clinicians involved in my care by screening everyone involved and were able to tie at least (1) independent contractor to my case and preselected the "fall guy" based on the independent contractor clause and exemption. This is how the VA Office of General Counsel gained the upper hand.

They repeatedly fed my family and I false hope and promises only to pull the rug right out from under our feet, denying our claim based on a "technicality" and an employment status, and left us holding the bag with no viable recourse, accountability or due process. This delayed notification of fault, combined with the FTCA exclusion of independent contractors, provided the agency with the perfect black hole through which medical malpractice claims disappear forever, no matter how egregious the wrong is or how badly it has ruined lives.

The "VA Independent Contractors" are only labeled as such when they get in trouble. Why would they work in VA hospitals and clinics, wear VA badges, VA doctors coats, have VA business cards, see VA patients, and produce VA reports, and come to the same place of business every day, use supplies, copy machines, printers, have keys to the building and call themselves "independent." By definition this is classified as an "employee," but this is how the Office of General Counsel can effectively deny and deflect all liability away from the VA and place it directly on the backs of unidentified independent contractors. The way the VA protects the independent contractors is they withhold crucial information that would otherwise support the veterans claim and case, all while the clock is ticking. When the state statute of limitations runs out (expires), the VA attorneys will drop a letter denying everything they already admitted to and advise you to sue the said clinician(s) in state court.

By that time, you have zero recourse because the state statutes have completely expired. This is how they strip your right to due process. This formula also works very well with retaining these "independent contractors" because according to the VA books medical malpractice never occurred within the VA system thus blaming the independents. This practice also serves to "water down" the numbers the VA provides relating to annual medical malpractice numbers. In turn they are never reported to the National Practitioner Data Bank because there is now no record of it. And yes, the "Independent Contractor" the VA General

Counsel threw under the bus is still employed at the same VA and is considered to be in "good standing" with the VA and the State of California. A report that a VA whistleblower sent me shows there were numerous VA emergency room clinicians that failed to meet the standard of care and there was a clear breach in liability, not just a single "independent contractor" at fault.

My brother and I spoke with the chief counsel, as well as several other VA attorneys after my denials. They stated that it takes upwards of a year to find out the employment status of clinicians who have been accused of medical malpractice. That seems as if it should be the first box that is checked when receiving any tort claim. Or perhaps this is how they see their way out of these cases? They wear you down until you give up, and leave you holding the bag in a condition where your survivability has been greatly affected because the injuries that occurred now prevent you from securing gainful employment. I would bet there is a strong correlation here with veteran suicide as I was nearly a statistic myself because of the physical pain and trauma, depression, anxiety, and the helplessness that you encounter when dealing with the VA attorneys. Chief counsel also stated this has happened before and it will happen again with greater frequency due to an increase in independent contractors hired by the VA.

Because of this horrific nightmare and the number of other veterans who already have endured this type of egregious treatment, it was time for me to take action. As I began uncovering jaw-dropping information and started to connect the dots on how these cases were manipulated by VA attorneys, I embarked on a mission to change the very law that essentially ruined my life. I formed an online legislative team, and we drafted a bill, we call it the "Tally Bill" or H.R. 4526. To date we have had (3) House bills formally introduced, as well as (1) Senate companion bill, to H.R. 4526. Obviously, our work is being heard and members of Congress are realizing we must address and fix this issue ASAP as we have an estimated 8 million American Veterans who are enrolled in VA healthcare, and will remain at risk until we have law. This law, if passed, would protect all Veterans who seek treatment in every VA hospital and clinic regardless of the employment status of the clinician. It would effectively place the necessary safeguards that are needed to ensure veteran protection to include a clear path of legal recourse in a timely manner and force the VA Office of General Counsel to work in good faith with veterans who are victimized by medical errors.

This bi-partisan veteran legislation will ensure the rights and protections of all veterans and their families after falling victim to VA medical malpractice. The "Brian Tally VA Employment Transparency Act" was introduced in partnership with Congressman Mike Levin and Congressman Mark

Meadows. We have made extraordinary headway in Congress; however, our mission is not complete! We continue to fight and advocate daily to ensure we effectively close this 74-year VA legal loophole that has dishonored Veterans and their families for generations and will continue to do so until Congress acts and passes H.R. 4526. VA hospitals and clinics can no longer be the place where accountability goes to die. We owe it to our Veterans to fix this systemic problem once and for all.

Respectfully Submitted,
Brian J. Tally
US Marine Veteran / Veteran Advocate

Here is a statement that was released immediately following the House Veterans Affairs committee hearing.

Marine veteran Brian Tally, who nearly died because of medical malpractice and still feels its effects today, is championing multiple pieces of legislation in Congress to fight back. At a House Veterans Affairs Committee hearing Wednesday, members of Congress pushed VA leadership for answers and heard from representatives from the VA Inspector General and Government Accountability offices. The Veterans Affairs watchdogs and journalists have reported about veterans being hurt by or dying because of underqualified or negligent VA doctors and other medical providers for years.

"These reports are sickening," Rep. Chris Pappas, D-NH, said, adding that VA leaders have shown "disregard for patient safety risks…and ignored concerns raised by staff" about substandard care and mismanagement. Collectively, the recent string of cases "speaks to a wider problem" at VA, Pappas said, adding that he wanted to know "What red flags are VA's facilities missing or overlooking or choosing to ignore?" And this is not new territory for VA, Pappas said.

CHAPTER 18:

THE PUSH FOR A SENATE COMPANION BILL

IMMEDIATELY FOLLOWING THE CONGRESSIONAL HEARING ON H.R. 4526 in front of the House Committee on Veterans' Affairs, I began to reach out to dozens of senators; one in particular was Senator Thom Tillis of North Carolina. We had met with a legislative staffer of his on a previous trip to Washington, DC, that went very well, and since that initial meeting we had stayed in close contact and built a great working relationship.

Now that we had all the gears and wheels in motion, I thought it would be as great a time as ever to have a Senate companion to H.R. 4526 formally introduced in the Senate to begin our simultaneous push for the successful passage of the Tally Bill both in the House and the Senate.

Of the other dozen or so US senators my team and I contacted; we came across a senator that was extremely interested in introducing the Senate companion bill we needed. Senator Richard Blumenthal of Connecticut was eager and ready to go. At that time, I was able to successfully connect the Republican Senator Tillis with the Democrat Senator Blumenthal, and on November 10, 2020, on the Marine Corps birthday, they co-introduced bicameral legislation, and Senate Bill 4883 was born. S.B. 4883 was a Senate companion bill to H.R. 4526. Here is the Senate bill language and what the law would do.

116TH CONGRESS
2D SESSION

S. 4883

To direct the Secretary of Veterans Affairs to provide certain notice to a person filing a claim against the Department of Veterans Affairs for damage, injury, or death on Standard Form 95, and for other purposes.

IN THE SENATE OF THE UNITED STATES

November 10, 2020

Mr. Blumenthal (for himself and Mr. Tillis) introduced the following bill: which was read twice and referred to the Committee on Veterans' Affairs

---

A BILL

To direct the Secretary of Veterans Affairs to provide certain notice to a person filing a claim against the Department of Veterans Affairs for damage, injury, or death on Standard Form 95, and for other purposes.

Be it enacted by the Senate and House of Representatives of the United States of America in Congress assembled,

SECTION 1. SHORT TITLE.

This Act may be cited as the "Brian Tally VA Employment Transparency Act of 2020".

SEC. 2. DEPARTMENT OF VETERANS AFFAIRS REQUIREMENT TO PROVIDE CERTAIN NOTICE TO PERSONS FILING CLAIMS FOR DAMAGE, INJURY, OR DEATH ON STANDARD FORM 95.

Not later than 30 days after the date on which a person submits to the Secretary of Veterans Affairs a claim for damage, injury, or death on Standard Form 95, or any successor form, the Secretary shall provide to the claimant notice of each of the following:

(1) The importance of obtaining legal advice, including a recommendation that the claimant should secure legal counsel.

(2) The employment status of any individual listed on the form.

(3) If the claim involves a contractor that entered into an agreement with the Secretary, the importance of obtaining legal advice as to the statute of limitations regarding the claim in the State in which the claim arose.

We were now well on our way to achieving our goal and accomplishing our mission. Soon after the Senate bill introduction Senator Richard Blumenthal released a statement.

"This bipartisan, bicameral bill will rectify the VA's gross administrative neglect and restore legal options to our country's veterans when they are wronged by the VA or a VA contractor" – Senator Richard Blumenthal (D-CT)

"I am incredibly honored to have Senator Blumenthal take the Senate lead on this landmark Veteran legislation and introduce this extraordinary VA accountability and transparency bill that will protect all Veterans who seek treatment at VA Hospitals and Clinics," said Tally.

"We have energetically and positively engaged Congress and have sought out motivated members of the Senate to be a Champion for all Veterans. We are honored that Senators Blumenthal and Tillis have both answered this call to service, in a bi-partisan fashion. They are playing a monumental role in effectively closing a 74-year VA legal loophole that has destroyed the lives of Veterans and their families for generations!"

"I look forward to working with the Senate VA Committee, Senate Republicans, and Senate Democrats to ensure the successful passage of the *Brian Tally VA Employment Transparency Act*. Together as one, we can, and we will see this through!"

Senator Tillis and Blumenthal's legislation would require that, within 30 days of a claim being filed, the VA notify the veteran filing the claim about the importance of getting legal counsel and the employment status of the person they are filing the claim against. If this person is a contractor, the VA would also need to inform the veteran about the importance of obtaining legal advice as to the statute of limitations in the state in which the claim arose. This bill is a companion to bipartisan legislation introduced in the U.S. House of Representatives in September 2019, led by U.S. Representatives Mike Levin (D-CA) and Mark Meadows (R-NC).

Now that we had made tremendous progress, and significant strides were made, we were now well on our way to having law and achieving this nearly impossible task in the most divided Congress in the history of the United States of America. I was immensely proud to have brought together some heavy hitters, and on a bipartisan level. The stage was set, and it was time to capitalize on our success and finish the job!

Tides were beginning to turn as we started winning these barrages of battles, and each day we accomplished more and more as our small steps over the years began to turn into giant monumental leaps towards restoring faith in the VA system.

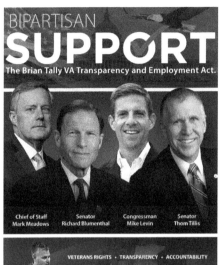

However, our legislative days were dwindling down, and the presidential election grew closer and closer as the congressional infighting became uglier and uglier in a time when we so desperately needed both sides to come together for the good of the country and pass this bill that would essentially close this seventy-four-year VA legal loophole that has destroyed the lives of veterans and their families for generations.

I had to remain steadfast in my resolve, fully engaged, and in front of the congressional members and their staff every day to remind them that we were so close, and that twenty million American veterans remained at risk, and that I did not have the energy to start all over for a third time in the 117th Congress!

We needed to get this job done now. I made a strong and final push on social media as my team of volunteers from across the country continually reached out to their elected officials, demanding change and to get the Tally Bill successfully across the finish line. We were so close I could feel it, and I continued to push as hard as I ever have, and I knew victory was imminent.

This was one of the many social media posts of mine that highlighted just how far we have come in our efforts in changing an outdated law that has dishonored veterans and their families for generations.

"Our tireless work, dedication, and commitment to this cause is nearing the finish line, and I am confident that we will soon have law. However, our work is not done!!

The mission has been clear, concise, consistent, and positive from the very beginning, and that is protecting all veterans who seek treatment at all VA hospitals and clinics. It all boiled down to transparency and accountability measures."

This was citizen and veteran advocacy at work, making a difference not only in our Country, but in the lives of all veterans.

I continued to encourage my friends, family, and supporters from across the country to please continue reaching out to your elected members of Congress and ask that they support, and pass H.R. 4526 and S.B. 4883 without further delay to ensure the rights and protections of all veterans!

I also closed with a motivating, "Let's get this job done, and finish strong!"

The media began to update my story and drive further awareness, as well as highlight all of the recent milestones and recap all that had happened over the years to get to this monumental point in this ever-changing story and journey. The media was victorious in putting significant pressure on the House and Senate to include the Tally Bill legislation in the end-of-the-year omnibus package. An omnibus bill is a single document that is accepted in a single vote by a legislature and packages together several measures into one or combines diverse subjects. Because of their large size and scope, omnibus bills limit opportunities for debate and scrutiny.

Through intense negotiations and aggressive lobbying efforts, both VA committees from the House and Senate agreed to include the Tally Bill into the omnibus legislative package, and as fate would have it, the bill number to this omnibus bill was H.R. 7105. You heard it right. What were the odds to have been given the same original bill number? Do you understand how many things would have to line up over the course of an entire Congress to have that be our actual bill number that could essentially end up getting us a cross the finish line, closing this generational loophole, and passing the Tally Bill. There was no other way to explain it other than divine intervention, and it further proved, *you can't fight fate*. If you remember correctly, H.R.7105 was our original and very first bill number that was first introduced on our initial visit to Washington, DC back in 2018 in the 115th Congress. Now, as one of the final bill numbers in the 116th Congress, H.R.7105 would carry us through to our next big moment, and my legislative story would end up beginning and ending with the same exact bill number! Impossible, right? It was absolutely astonishing.

This was a complete and utter goose bumps moment for me as the hair on the back of my neck stood up and my heart beamed with pride and emotions as I fought back tears. It felt as if this journey was finally coming to an end, and all of the hard work, determination, dedication, and duty to our country was being heard, and now all we could do is sit back, wait, watch, and pray that this omnibus bill would pass both the House and the Senate.

Senator Richard Blumenthal (D-CT) stated in a press release after the bill was added to the omnibus package. "It is simply unacceptable that the VA is failing to properly notify our country's veterans about their options when they file legal claims, essentially robbing them of their rights. Veterans must have the ability to seek legal recourse in cases of medical malpractice or other negligence—period."

CHAPTER 19:
THE TALLY BILL BECOMES LAW

I WILL NEVER FORGET THE MOMENT ON THE NIGHT OF DECEMBER 9, 2020, as I laid in bed watching a late-night Senate session, when they brought the Tally Bill to the floor of the Senate, and it passed.

The only issue is that there were some slight amendments to the bill, and it would now have to pass the House again. Either way, it was exceedingly certain that we would soon have law.

On December 16, 2020, H.R. 7105 made its way back to the House floor for a final vote. This was literally on one of the last legislative days on the congressional calendar. It came all the way down to the wire. At that time, the House filed a motion to suspend the rules and agree to the Senate amendment that was put forth a week ago and agreed to by a voice vote.

The bill passed unanimously, and we now had successful passage of the Tally Bill in both chambers, and it was presented to President Donald J. Trump on December 24, 2020. Any time a bill passes and heads to the president's desk for signature, there is only ten working days for the president to sign it after it has been presented by Congress.

If the bill goes unsigned, it essentially dies in Congress, the bill becomes null and void, and the process would have started all over. The good news was the White House had no objection to the bill. After all, one of our biggest advocates and allies of the Tally Bill was now the chief of staff for President Trump. However, we were delayed and pushed out all the way to the ten-day mark as distractions and wall to wall coverage of breaking news stories filled the attention of the president and his staff.

On January 5, 2021, on the final day, which was the tenth business day, every veterans group and veterans advocates from across the country, including myself, waited and watched on pins and needles for any developments on when President Trump would be signing the omnibus bill, which was H.R. 7105 and included the Tally Bill, into law. Finally, the call that I had been waiting for came, and the years of pain, blood, sweat, and tears that put me on my knees were signed into law, closing a seventy-four-year VA legal loophole that has destroyed the lives of veterans and their families for generations!

My life has changed in ways I could have never seen coming or ever imagined. The injustices that my family and I faced during our darkest hour of physical, emotional, and mental pain came and were orchestrated from the highest levels of the Department of Veterans Affairs.

What happened to my family and me and the countless other veterans before us was downright frightening, unconstitutional, and criminal. I knew something needed to be done, so I made it my life goal to change federal law to ensure the rights and protections of all veterans! I honorably and positively engaged Congress and delivered a solution to a generational loophole.

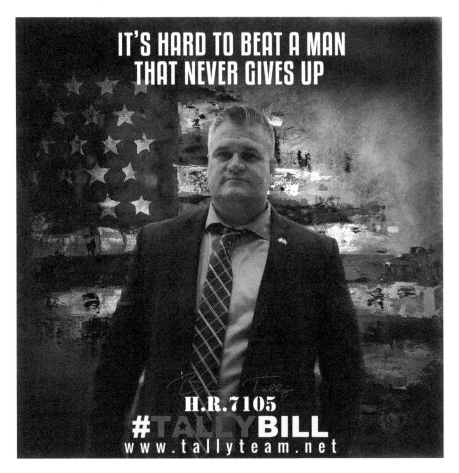

From this point forward, all veterans and their families will now have the accountability and transparency they deserve in a timely manner from the highest levels of the Department of Veterans Affairs after falling victim to VA medical malpractice.

The new rules are not retroactive, so my family and I will not directly benefit from the law change; however, having my last name forever inked into federal law, and being responsible for a grassroots effort that sparked an act of Congress to pass landmark and monumental legislation, is all I need, and I have considered this my settlement.

My family and I are now residing in Texas and have started our next chapter in life. Here is a recent family photo. I am a blessed man!

My goal from the very beginning was to create positive change and give all veterans a clear path of legal recourse after their lives fall apart due to no fault of their own. I also prayed for and dreamed of a happy ending, and to essentially turn a negative into a positive, and I did just that.

In closing, I am exhausted, relieved, and proud all at the same time to have finally crossed the finish line and received this much-needed mental closure. This is what my family and I have longed for, to effectively close out this egregious five-year chapter, turn the page, and move on with our lives knowing this will never happen again and ruin the lives of other veterans and their families.

MISSION ACCOMPLISHED!

"I DIDN'T CHOOSE THIS JOB, IT CHOSE ME!"

THE END

CPSIA information can be obtained
at www.ICGtesting.com
Printed in the USA
JSHW051917281022
32219JS00006B/22